Principles of Package Design
Creating Reusable Software Components

Matthias Noback

Apress®

Principles of Package Design: Creating Reusable Software Components

Matthias Noback
Zeist, The Netherlands

ISBN-13 (pbk): 978-1-4842-4118-9   ISBN-13 (electronic): 978-1-4842-4119-6
https://doi.org/10.1007/978-1-4842-4119-6

Library of Congress Control Number: 2018962262

Managing Director, Apress Media LLC: Welmoed Spahr
Acquisitions Editor: Shiva Ramachandran
Development Editor: Laura Berendson
Coordinating Editor: Rita Fernando

Cover designed by eStudioCalamar

Cover image designed by Freepik (www.freepik.com)

Distributed to the book trade worldwide by Springer Science+Business Media New York, 233 Spring Street, 6th Floor, New York, NY 10013. Phone 1-800-SPRINGER, fax (201) 348-4505, e-mail orders-ny@springer-sbm.com, or visit www.springeronline.com. Apress Media, LLC is a California LLC and the sole member (owner) is Springer Science + Business Media Finance Inc (SSBM Finance Inc). SSBM Finance Inc is a **Delaware** corporation.

For information on translations, please e-mail rights@apress.com, or visit http://www.apress.com/rights-permissions.

Apress titles may be purchased in bulk for academic, corporate, or promotional use. eBook versions and licenses are also available for most titles. For more information, reference our Print and eBook Bulk Sales web page at http://www.apress.com/bulk-sales.

Any source code or other supplementary material referenced by the author in this book is available to readers on GitHub via the book's product page, located at www.apress.com/9781484241189. For more detailed information, please visit http://www.apress.com/source-code.

Printed on acid-free paper

To Lies, Lucas, & Julia

Table of Contents

About the Author

Matthias Noback is a professional PHP developer. He runs his own web development, training, and consultancy company called Noback's Office. In the past, he has worked as a software developer at Driebit (Amsterdam) and IPPZ (Utrecht), and as a CTO at Ibuildings (Utrecht). Since 2011, he has been regularly writing on his blog (matthiasnoback.nl) about advanced software development-related topics. His favorite topics are software architecture, legacy code, testing, and object design. Other books by the author are *A Year with Symfony* and *Microservices for Everyone*. You can find him on Twitter as @matthiasnoback.

About the Technical Reviewer

Ross Tuck is a software engineer and coach. He speaks about software development at conferences around the world and is a frequent contributor to podcasts, articles, and occasionally GitHub Repos. Originally from the United States, he now lives in the Netherlands with his wife and cat. You can find him on Twitter as @rosstuck.

Acknowledgments

A quick word of thanks to some people in particular. First of all, to Robert C. Martin. Many of the design principles covered in this book originate from his work.

There were many people who provided some valuable feedback based on their proofreading of the first edition, like Brian Fenton, Kevin Archer, Luis Cordova, Mark Badolato, Matthijs van Rietschoten, Ramon de la Fuente, Richard Perez, Rolf Babijn, Sebastian Stok, Thomas Shone, and Peter Rehm. One of the proofreaders that I want to mention in particular is Peter Bowyer, who offered many detailed suggestions. He also did the brilliant suggestion to turn this initially PHP-specific book into something that is interesting and useful for *every* software developer.

Even though this book is language-agnostic, I owe a lot to the particular community to which I belong: the PHP community. Thank you all for being awesome—providing great reading material, insights, friendly invitations, and lots of good code—on a daily basis.

A big "thank you" goes out to Ross Tuck, who performed a thorough technical review of the second edition of this book. Although he certainly provided me with a lot of extra work, I'm extremely happy that he did. He pointed out many things I could do to make the book more useful and understandable for a broad range of people, with different perspectives and different experiences in the field.

Thanks to Apress—in particular Shiva, Laura, and Rita—for adopting the *Principles of Package Design* and creating the opportunity to release it in a much better shape, and at the same time making it available to many more readers.

Finally, thank you Lies, Lucas, and Julia. Thank you for letting me step away from family business and write this book in solitude. And thank you for always embracing me when I stepped back in.

Introduction

While writing this book, I assumed that you, the reader, are a programmer who uses an object-oriented programming language to create applications. This means that you have some experience creating classes, methods, interfaces, etc. and are trying to make all of these things work well together. While you know how to do that, you may also be wondering from time to time: "Am I doing this right?"

It's not a bad question, and certainly an understandable one. As a programmer, you have to make so many choices in a single working day; it's only natural to worry if you're making all the right decisions. A bad decision today could lead to a lot of extra work later.

Unfortunately, there's no way to know for sure if you're doing it right. The best thing you can do is keep an eye on how things evolve and be ready to change course when needed. But to train your eye and learn to predict where things will be heading, you should also tap into other sources. For instance, you could read a book on programming. Or you could learn from another programmer's experience.

When I started to open source some code that I thought would be useful for other programmers, I also regularly wondered: "Am I doing this right?" I went to look for sources that I could learn from. For class design, there are an awful lot of online and offline sources. Way more than there are about package design. I couldn't find a lot of material that would help me do a better job at creating packages, except for a few book sections (never an entire book) and some old articles.

One recurring source was Robert C. Martin's website butunclebob.com, which features some articles about the SOLID principles of class design, and two articles about *component design principles*. In these articles, Robert provides some very straightforward design principles for reusable components. When I first read them, it was immediately clear to me that every programmer should know about them. So I started writing this book, elaborating on these principles, and explaining them in the context of creating reusable and distributable software components, also known as "packages". The package design principles provide an answer to the following questions:

- Which classes belong inside a package and which don't?

- Which packages are safe to depend on and which aren't?

- What can I do for my users to enhance the usability of a package?

- What can I do for myself to keep a package maintainable?

If you're interested in creating your own (not necessarily open source) packages, knowing these answers will help you do a good job from the start. The principles will be a guiding help along the way. If you have already created some packages, knowing these principles will help you make your next release even better.

If, on the other hand, you're not at all interested in developing packages, you'll still gain a lot useful insights from this book. First, because the book also provides many clues about good class design. Second, because these package design principles will help structure any software project, whether that be a reusable library, some standalone component, or even an entire module within an application. This book offers many useful techniques for organizing your code into groups of any size.

Overview of the Contents

The majority of this book covers package design principles. But first we must consider the contents of a package: classes and interfaces. The way you design them has great consequences for the characteristics of the package in which they will eventually reside. So, before considering package design principles themselves, we first need to take a look at the principles of class design. These are the so-called *SOLID* principles. Each letter of this acronym stands for a different principle, and we will briefly revisit them in the first part of this book.

The second part of the book covers the six major principles of package design. The first three are about *cohesion*. While class cohesion is about which *methods* belong inside a *class*, package cohesion is about which *classes* belong inside a *package*. The *package cohesion* principles tell you which classes should be put together in a package, when to split packages, and if a combination of classes may be considered a "package" in the first place.

The second three package design principles are about *coupling*. Coupling is important at the class level, since most classes are pretty useless on their own. They need other classes with which to collaborate. Class design principles like the *Dependency Inversion* principle help you write nicely decoupled classes. But when the dependencies of a class lie outside its own package, you need a way to determine if it's safe to couple the package to another package. The *package coupling* principles will help you choose the right dependencies. They will also help you recognize and prevent wrong directions in the dependency graph of your packages.

Notes About the Code Samples

Although I wanted this book to be useful for any programmer, the code samples themselves still needed to be written in a particular language. I chose PHP, because it's the programming language I know best, which is convenient for me. If you don't know PHP, it shouldn't be a problem to understand the code, as long as you're familiar with some other object-oriented programming language.

Be aware that the sample code isn't exactly production-ready. It's only there to bring across some technical points. You shouldn't copy/paste it into your projects.

To simplify the code samples and point out the areas that matter most, I've established the following conventions:

- I abbreviate property and method declarations using //...

- I abbreviate expressions using ...

- When an example shows the same code again, but modified, I repeat as little of the original code as possible.

- Although I don't consider using the "Interface" suffix to be a best practice, I'll still do it in the code samples, because it makes it easier to talk about interfaces in the regular text.

- Although I do consider it best practice to declare classes as "final" (I'll explain why later), I won't do it in most of the code samples, because it can be a bit of a distraction.

PART I

Class Design

Developers like you and I need help making our decisions: we have incredibly many choices to make, each day, all day. So if there are some principles we think are sound, we happily follow them. Principles are guidelines, or "things you should do". There is no real imperative there. You are not *required* to follow these principles, but in theory you *should*.

When it comes to creating classes, there are many guidelines you should follow, like: choose descriptive names, keep the number of variables low, use few control structures, etc. But these are actually quite general programming guidelines. They will keep your code readable, understandable, and therefore maintainable. Also, they are quite specific, so your team may be very strict about them ("at most two levels of indentation inside each method," "at most three instance variables", etc.).

Next to these general programming guidelines there are also some deeper principles that can be applied to class design. These are powerful principles, but less specific in most cases, and it is therefore much harder to be strict about them. Each of these principles brings some room for discussion. Also, not all of them can or should be applied all the time. (Unlike the more general programming guidelines—when not applied, your code will most certainly start to get in your way pretty soon.)

The principles I refer to are named the "*SOLID*" principles, a term coined by Robert Martin. In the following chapters, I give a brief summary of each of these principles. Even though the SOLID principles are concerned with the design of classes, a discussion of them belongs in this book, since the class design principles resonate with the package design principles we discuss in the second part of this book.

Why Follow the Principles?

When you learn about the SOLID principles, you may ask yourself: why do I have to stay true to them? Take for example the *Open/Closed* principle: "You should be able to extend the behavior of a class without modifying it." Why, actually? Is it so bad to change the behavior of a class by opening its file in an editor and making some changes? Or take for instance the *Dependency Inversion* principle, which says: "Depend on abstractions, not on concretions." Why again? What's wrong with depending on concretions?

Of course, in the following chapters I take great care in explaining to you why you should use these principles and what happens if you don't. But to make this clear before you take the dive: the SOLID principles for class design are there to prepare your codebase for future changes. You want these changes to be local, not global, and small, not big.

Prepare for Change

Why do you want to make as few and as little changes as possible to existing code? First of all, there is the risk of one of those changes breaking the entire system. Then there is the amount of time you need to invest for each change in an existing class—to understand what it originally does, and where best to add or remove some lines of code. But there is also the extra burden in modifying the existing unit tests for the class. Besides, each change may be part of some review process. It may require a rebuild of the entire system, or it may even require others to update their systems to reflect the changes.

This would almost lead us to the conclusion that changing existing code is something we don't want. However, to dismiss change in general would be way too much. Most real businesses change heavily over time, and so do their software requirements. So to keep functioning as a software developer, you need to *embrace change* yourself too. And to make it easier for you to cope with the quickly changing requirements, you need to prepare your code for them. Luckily, there are many ways to accomplish that, which can all be extracted from the following five SOLID class design principles.

## CHAPTER 1

The Single Responsibility Principle

The *Single Responsibility* principle says that[1]:

> *A class should have one, and only one, reason to change.*

There is a strange little jump here, from this principle being about "responsibilities" to the explanation being about "reasons to change". Well, this is not so strange when you think about it—each responsibility is also a reason to change.

A Class with Too Many Responsibilities

Let's take a look at a concrete, probably recognizable example of a class that is used to send a confirmation to the email address of a new user (see Listing 1-1 and Figure 1-1). It has some dependencies, like a templating engine for rendering the body of the email message, a translator for translating the message's subject, and a mailer for sending the message. These are all injected by their interface (which is good; see Chapter 5).

---

[1]Robert C. Martin, "The Principles of OOD," `http://butunclebob.com/ArticleS.UncleBob.` `PrinciplesOfOod`

© Matthias Noback 2018
M. Noback, *Principles of Package Design*, https://doi.org/10.1007/978-1-4842-4119-6_1

Listing 1-1. The ConfirmationMailMailer Class

```
class ConfirmationMailMailer
{
    private $templating;
    private $translator;
    private $mailer;

    public function __construct(
        TemplatingEngineInterface $templating,
        TranslatorInterface $translator,
        MailerInterface $mailer
    ) {
        $this->templating = $templating;
        $this->translator = $translator;
        $this->mailer = $mailer;
    }

    public function sendTo(User $user): void
    {
        $message = $this->createMessageFor($user);

        $this->sendMessage($message);
    }

    private function createMessageFor(User $user): Message
    {
        $subject = $this
            ->translator
            ->translate('Confirm your mail address');

        $body = $this
            ->templating
            ->render('confirmationMail.html.tpl', [
                'confirmationCode' => $user->getConfirmationCode()
            ]);
```

```
    $message = new Message($subject, $body);

    $message->setTo($user->getEmailAddress());

    return $message;
  }

  private function sendMessage(Message $message): void
  {
    $this->mailer->send($message);
  }
}
```

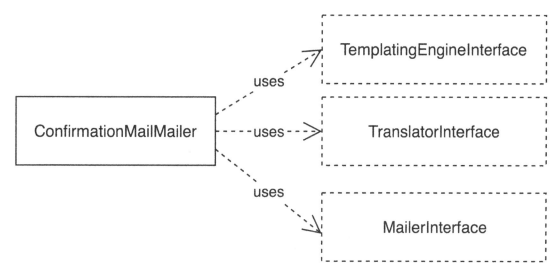

Figure 1-1. *A diagram of the initial situation*

Responsibilities Are Reasons to Change

When you talk to someone about this class, you would say that it has two jobs, or two responsibilities—to *create* a confirmation mail and to *send* it. These two responsibilities are also its two reasons to change. Whenever the requirements change regarding the creation of the message or regarding the sending of the message, this class will have to be modified. This also means that when either of the responsibilities requires a change, the *entire* class needs to be opened and modified, while most of it may have nothing to do with the requested change itself.

Since changing existing code is something that needs to be prevented, or at least be confined (see the Introduction), and responsibilities are reasons to change, we should try to minimize the number of responsibilities of each class. This would at the same time minimize the chance that the class has to be opened for modification.

Because a class with no responsibilities is a useless class, the best we can do with regard to minimizing the number of responsibilities is reduce it to one. Hence, the *Single Responsibility* principle.

RECOGNIZING VIOLATIONS OF THE *SINGLE RESPONSIBILITY* PRINCIPLE

This is a list of symptoms of a class that may violate the *Single Responsibility* principle:

- The class has many instance variables.

- The class has many public methods.

- Each method of the class uses different instance variables.

- Specific tasks are delegated to private methods.

These are all good reasons to extract so-called "collaborator classes" from the class, thereby delegating some of the class' responsibilities and making it adhere to the *Single Responsibility* principle.

Refactoring: Using Collaborator Classes

We now know that the ConfirmationMailMailer does too many things and is therefore a liability. The way we can (and in this case should) refactor the class is by extracting collaborator classes. Since this class is a "mailer," we let it keep the responsibility of *sending the message* to the user. But we extract the responsibility of *creating the message*.

Creating a message is a bit more complicated than a simple object instantiation using the new operator. It even requires several dependencies. This calls for a dedicated "factory" class—the ConfirmationMailFactory class (see Listing 1-2 and Figure 1-2).

Listing 1-2. The ConfirmationMailFactory Class

```php
class ConfirmationMailMailer
{
    private $confirmationMailFactory;
    private $mailer;

    public function __construct(
        ConfirmationMailFactory $confirmationMailFactory
        MailerInterface $mailer
    ) {
        $this->confirmationMailFactory = $confirmationMailFactory;
        $this->mailer = $mailer;
    }

    public function sendTo(User $user): void
    {
        $message = $this->createMessageFor($user);

        $this->sendMessage($message);
    }

    private function createMessageFor(User $user): Message
    {
        return $this->confirmationMailFactory
                    ->createMessageFor($user);
    }

    private function sendMessage(Message $message): void
    {
        $this->mailer->send($message);
    }
}

class ConfirmationMailFactory
{
    private $templating;
    private $translator;
```

```php
public function __construct(
    TemplatingEngineInterface $templating,
    TranslatorInterface $translator
) {
    $this->templating = $templating;
    $this->translator = $translator;
}

public function createMessageFor(User $user): Message
{
    /*
     * Create an instance of Message based on the
     * given User
     */
    $message = ...;

    return $message;
}
}
```

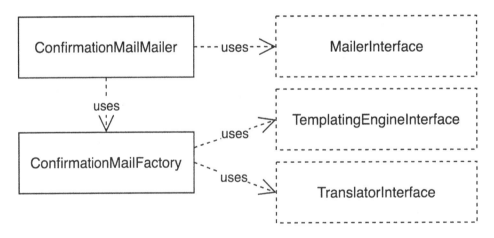

Figure 1-2. *Introducing the ConfirmationMailFactory class*

Now the creation logic of the confirmation mail has been nicely placed inside
ConfirmationMailFactory. It would be even better if an interface was defined for the
factory class, but it's fine for now.

Advantages of Having a Single Responsibility

As a side effect of the refactoring to single responsibilities, both of the classes are easier to test. You can now test both responsibilities separately. The correctness of the created message can be verified by testing the `createMessageFor()` method of `ConfirmationMailFactory`. Testing the `sendTo()` method of `ConfirmationMailMailer` is also quite easy now, because you can mock up the complete message-creation process and just focus on sending the message.

In general, you will notice that classes with single responsibilities are easier to test. Having a single responsibility will make a class smaller, so you have to write fewer tests to keep that class covered. This will be easier for your mind to grasp. Also, these small classes will have fewer private methods with effects that need to be verified in a unit test.

Finally, smaller classes are also simpler to maintain. It is easier to grasp their purpose and all the implementation details are where they belong: in the classes responsible for them.

Packages and the Single Responsibility Principle

While the *Single Responsibility* principle should be applied to classes, in a slightly different way it should also be applied to groups of classes (also known as *packages*). In the context of package design, "having only one reason to change" becomes "being closed against the same kind of changes". The corresponding package principle is called the *Common Closure* principle (see Chapter 8).

A somewhat exaggerated example of a package that doesn't follow this *Common Closure* principle would be a package that knows how to connect with a MySQL database *and* knows how to produce HTML pages. Such a package would have too many responsibilities and will be opened (i.e., modified) for all sorts of reasons. The solution for packages like this one is to split them into smaller packages, each with fewer responsibilities, and therefore fewer reasons to change.

There is another interesting similarity between the *Single Responsibility* principle of class design and the *Common Closure* principle of package design that I'd like to quickly mention here: following these principles in most cases reduces class (and package) coupling.

When a class has many *responsibilities*, it is likely to have many *dependencies* too. It probably gets many objects injected as constructor arguments to be able to fulfill its goal. For example, `ConfirmationMailMailer` needed a translator service, a templating engine, and a mailer to create and send a confirmation mail. By depending on those objects, it was directly coupled to them. When we applied the *Single Responsibility* principle and moved the responsibility of creating the message to a new class called `ConfirmationMailFactory`, we reduced the number of dependencies of `ConfirmationMailMailer` and thereby reduced its coupling.

The same goes for the *Common Closure* principle. When a package has many dependencies, it is tightly coupled to each of them, which means that a change in one of the dependencies will likely require a change in the package too. Applying the *Common Closure* principle to a package means reducing the number of reasons for a package to change. Removing dependencies, or deferring them to other packages, is one way to accomplish this.

Conclusion

Every class has responsibilities, i.e. things to do. Responsibilities are also reasons for change. The *Single Responsibility* principle tells us to limit the number of responsibilities of each class, in order to minimize the number of reasons for a class to be changed.

Limiting the number of responsibilities usually leads to the extraction of one or more collaborating classes. Each of these classes will have a smaller number of dependencies. This is useful for package development, since every class will be easier to instantiate, test, and use.

## CHAPTER 2

The Open/Closed Principle

The *Open/Closed* principle says that[1]:

> *You should be able to extend a class's behavior without modifying it.*

Again, a small linguistic jump has to be made from the name of the principle to its explanation: a unit of code can be considered "open for extension" when its behavior can be easily changed *without* modifying it. The fact that no actual modification is needed to change the behavior of a unit of code makes it "closed" for modification.

It should be noted that being able to extend a class's behavior doesn't mean you should actually *extend* that class by creating a subclass for it. Extension of a class means that you can influence its behavior from the outside and leave the class, or the entire class hierarchy, untouched.

A Class That Is Closed for Extension

Take a look at the GenericEncoder class shown in Listing 2-1 and Figure 2-1. Notice the branching inside the encodeToFormat() method that is needed to choose the right encoder based on the value of the $format argument.

---

[1]Robert C. Martin, "The Principles of OOD," `http://butunclebob.com/ArticleS.UncleBob.PrinciplesOfOod`.

© Matthias Noback 2018
M. Noback, *Principles of Package Design*, https://doi.org/10.1007/978-1-4842-4119-6_2

Listing 2-1. The GenericEncoder Class

```
class GenericEncoder
{
    public function encodeToFormat($data, string $format): string
    {
        if ($format === 'json') {
            $encoder = new JsonEncoder();
        } elseif ($format === 'xml') {
            $encoder = new XmlEncoder();
        } else {
            throw new InvalidArgumentException('Unknown format');
        }

        $data = $this->prepareData($data, $format);

        return $encoder->encode($data);
    }
}
```

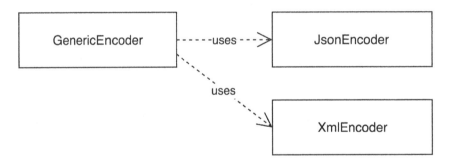

Figure 2-1. *The initial situation*

Let's say you want to use the GenericEncoder to encode data to the Yaml format, which is currently not supported by the encoder. The obvious solution would be to create a YamlEncoder class for this purpose and then add an extra condition inside the existing encodeToFormat() method shown in Listing 2-2.

Listing 2-2. Adding Another Encoding Format

```
class GenericEncoder
{
    public function encodeToFormat($data, string $format): string
    {
        if (...) {
            // ...
        } elseif (...) {
            // ...
        } elseif ($format === 'yaml') {
            $encoder = new YamlEncoder();
        } else {
            // ...
        }

        // ...
    }
}
```

As you can imagine, each time you want to add another format-specific encoder, the GenericEncoder class itself needs to be *modified:* you cannot change its behavior without modifying its code. This is why the GenericEncoder class cannot be considered *open for extension* and *closed for modification.*

Let's take a look at the prepareData() method of the same class. Just like the encodeToFormat() method, it contains some more format-specific logic (see Listing 2-3).

Listing 2-3. The prepareData() Method

```
class GenericEncoder
{
    public function encodeToFormat($data, string $format): string
    {
        // ...

        $data = $this->prepareData($data, $format);

        // ...
    }
```

13

```php
    private function prepareData($data, string $format)
    {
        switch ($format) {
            case 'json':
                $data = $this->forceArray($data);
                $data = $this->fixKeys($data);
                // fall through
            case 'xml':
                $data = $this->fixAttributes($data);
                break;
            default:
                throw new InvalidArgumentException(
                    'Format not supported'
                );
        }

        return $data;
    }
}
```

The prepareData() method is another good example of code that is *closed for extension* since it is *impossible* to add support for another format without modifying the code itself. Besides, these kind of switch statements are not good for maintainability. When you would have to modify this code, for instance when you introduce a new format, it is likely that you would either introduce some code duplication or simply make a mistake because you overlooked the "fall-through" case.

RECOGNIZING CLASSES THAT VIOLATE THE OPEN/CLOSED PRINCIPLE

This is a list of characteristics of a class that may not be open for extension:

- It contains conditions to determine a strategy.

- Conditions using the same variables or constants are recurring inside the class or related classes.

- The class contains hard-coded references to other classes or class names.

- Inside the class, objects are being created using the new operator.

- The class has protected properties or methods, to allow changing its behavior by overriding state or behavior.

Refactoring: Abstract Factory

We'd like to fix this bad design, which requires us to constantly dive into the GenericEncoder class to modify format-specific behavior. We first need to delegate the responsibility of resolving the right encoder for the format to some other class. When you think of responsibilities as reasons to change (see Chapter 1), this makes perfect sense: the logic for finding the right format-specific encoder is something which is likely to change, so it would be good to transfer this responsibility to another class.

This new class might as well be an implementation of the *Abstract Factory* design pattern[2]. The abstractness is represented by the fact that its create() method is bound to return an instance of a given *interface*. We don't care about its actual class; we only want to retrieve an object with an encode($data) method. So we need an interface for such format-specific encoders. And then, we make sure every existing format-specific encoder implements this interface (see Listing 2-4 and Figure 2-2).

Listing 2-4. The EncoderInterface and Its Implementation Classes

```
/**
 * Interface for format-specific encoders
 */
interface EncoderInterface
{
    public function encode($data): string;
}

class JsonEncoder implements EncoderInterface
{
    // ...
}
```

---

[2]Erich Gamma e.a., *Design Patterns: Elements of Reusable Object-Oriented Software*, Addison-Wesley, 1994.

```
class XmlEncoder implements EncoderInterface
{
    // ...
}

class YamlEncoder implements EncoderInterface
{
    // ...
}
```

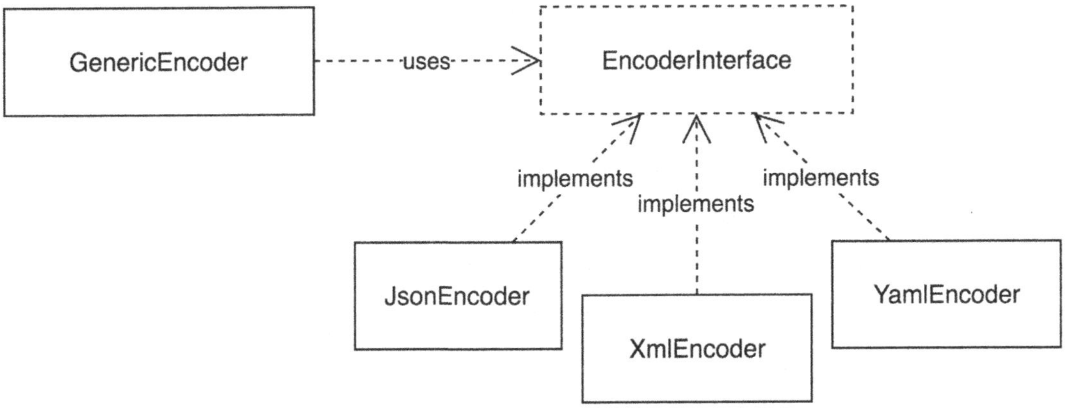

Figure 2-2. *Introducing the EncoderInterface*

Now we can move the creation logic of format-specific encoders to a class with just this responsibility. Let's call it EncoderFactory (see Listing 2-5).

Listing 2-5. The EncoderFactory Class

```
class EncoderFactory
{
    public function createForFormat(
        string $format
    ) : EncoderInterface {
        if ($format === 'json') {
            return new JsonEncoder();
        } elseif ($format === 'xml') {
            return new XmlEncoder();
```

```
    } elseif (...) {
        // ...
    }

    throw new InvalidArgumentException('Unknown format');
    }
}
```

Then we have to make sure that the GenericEncoder class does not create any format-specific encoders anymore. Instead, it should delegate this job to the EncoderFactory class, which it receives as a constructor argument (see Listing 2-6).

Listing 2-6. The GenericEncoder Class Now Uses EncoderFactory

```
class GenericEncoder
{
    private $encoderFactory;

    public function __construct(
        EncoderFactory $encoderFactory
    ) {
        $this->encoderFactory = $encoderFactory;
    }

    public function encodeToFormat($data, string $format): string
    {
        $encoder = $this->encoderFactory
                        ->createForFormat($format);

        $data = $this->prepareData($data, $format);

        return $encoder->encode($data);
    }
}
```

By leaving the responsibility of creating the right encoder to the encoder factory, the GenericEncoder now conforms to the *Single Responsibility* principle.

Using the encoder factory for fetching the right encoder for a given format means that adding an extra format-specific encoder *does not require us to modify* the GenericEncoder class anymore. We need to modify the EncoderFactory class instead.

But when we look at the EncoderFactory class, there is still an ugly hard-coded list of supported formats and their corresponding encoders. Even worse, class names are still hard-coded. This means that now the EncoderFactory is *closed against extension.* That is, its behavior can't be extended without modifying its code. It thereby violates the *Open/Closed* principle.

QUICK REFACTORING OPPORTUNITY: DYNAMIC CLASS NAMES?

It seems there is some low-hanging fruit here. As you may have noticed there is a striking symmetry inside the switch statement: for the json format, a JsonEncoder instance is being returned, for the xml format an XmlEncoder, etc. If your programming language supports dynamic class names, like PHP does, this could be easily refactored into something that is not hard-coded anymore:

```
$class = ucfirst(strtolower($format)) . 'Encoder';
if (!class_exists($class)) {
    throw new InvalidArgumentException('Unknown format');
}
```

Yes, this is in fact equivalent code. It's shorter and it removes the need for a switch statement. It even introduces a bit more flexibility: in order to extend its behavior you don't need to modify the code anymore. In the case of the new encoder for the Yaml format, we only need to create a new class that follows the naming convention: YamlEncoder. And that's it. However, using dynamic class names to make a class extensible like this introduces some new problems and doesn't fix some of the existing problems:

- Introducing a naming convention only offers some flexibility for you as the maintainer of the code. When someone else wants to add support for a new format, they have to put a class in your namespace, which is possible, but not really user-friendly.

- A much bigger issue: creation logic is still being reduced to new ...(). If, for instance, an encoder class has some dependencies, there is no way to inject them (e.g., as constructor arguments). We will address this issue next.

Refactoring: Making the Abstract Factory Open for Extension

A first step we could take is to apply the *Dependency Inversion* principle (see Chapter 5) by defining an interface for encoder factories. The EncoderFactory we already have should implement this new interface and the constructor argument of the GenericEncoder should have the interface as its type (see Listing 2-7 and Figure 2-3).

Listing 2-7. An Interface for the Factory

```
interface EncoderFactoryInterface
{
    public function createForFormat(
        string $format
    ): EncoderInterface;
}

class EncoderFactory implements EncoderFactoryInterface
{
    // ...
}

class GenericEncoder
{
    public function __construct(
        EncoderFactoryInterface $encoderFactory
    ) {
        // ...
    }

    // ...
}
```

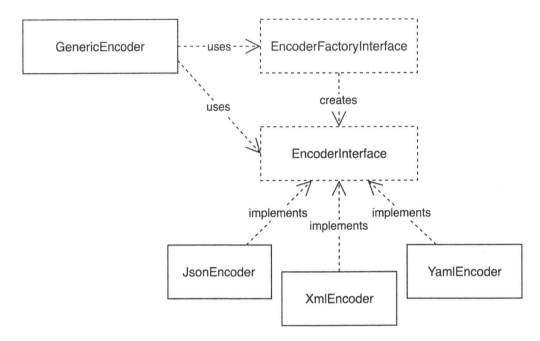

Figure 2-3. *Introducing the EncoderFactoryInterface*

Replacing or Decorating the Encoder Factory

By making GenericEncoder depend on an interface instead of a class, we have added a first extension point to it. It will be easy for users of this class to completely replace the encoder factory, which is now a proper dependency that gets injected as a constructor argument of type EncoderFactoryInterface (see Listing 2-8).

Listing 2-8. Replacing the Encoder Factory with a Custom One

```
class MyCustomEncoderFactory implements EncoderFactoryInterface
{
    // ...
}
$encoder = new GenericEncoder(new MyCustomEncoderFactory());
```

By introducing the interface, we've provided the user with another very powerful option. Maybe they aren't looking to completely replace the existing EncoderFactory, but they just want to enhance its behavior. For example, let's say they want to fetch the encoder for a given format from a service locator and fall back on the default EncoderFactory in case of an unknown format. Using the interface, they can *compose* a new factory, which implements the required interface, but receives the original EncoderFactory as a constructor argument (see Listing 2-9). You could say that the new factory "wraps" the old one. The technical term for this is "decoration".

Listing 2-9. Decorating the Original EncoderFactory

```php
class MyCustomEncoderFactory implements EncoderFactoryInterface
{
    private $fallbackFactory;
    private $serviceLocator;

    public function __construct(
        ServiceLocatorInterface $serviceLocator,
        EncoderFactoryInterface $fallbackFactory
    ) {
        $this->serviceLocator = $serviceLocator;
        $this->fallbackFactory = $fallbackFactory;
    }

    public function createForFormat($format): EncoderInterface
    {
        if ($this->serviceLocator->has($format . '.encoder') {
            return $this->serviceLocator
                        ->get($format . '.encoder');
        }

        return $this->fallbackFactory->createForFormat($format);
    }
}
```

Making EncoderFactory Itself Open for Extension

It's great that users can now implement their own instance of EncoderFactoryInterface or decorate an existing instance. However, forcing the user to re-implement EncoderFactoryInterface just to add support for another format seems a bit inefficient. When a new format comes along, we want to keep using the same old EncoderFactory, but we want to support the new format without touching the code of the class itself. Also, if one of the encoders would need another object to fulfill its task, it's currently not possible to provide that object as a constructor argument, because the *creation logic* of each of the encoders is hard-coded in the EncoderFactory class.

In other words, it's impossible to extend or change the behavior of the EncoderFactory class without modifying it: the logic by which the encoder factory decides which encoder it should create and how it should do that for any given format can't be changed from the outside. But it's quite easy to move this logic out of the EncoderFactory class, thereby making the class *open for extension*.

There are several ways to make a factory like EncoderFactory open for extension. I've chosen to inject specialized factories into the EncoderFactory, as shown in Listing 2-10.

Listing 2-10. Injecting Specialized Factories

```
class EncoderFactory implements EncoderFactoryInterface
{
    private $factories = [];

    /**
     * Register a callable that returns an instance of
     * EncoderInterface for the given format.
     *
     * @param string $format
     * @param callable $factory
     */

    public function addEncoderFactory(
        string $format,
        callable $factory
    ): void {
        $this->factories[$format] = $factory;
    }

    public function createForFormat(
        string $format
    ): EncoderInterface {
        $factory = $this->factories[$format];
```

```
        // the factory is a callable
        $encoder = $factory();

        return $encoder;
    }
}
```

For each format it is possible to inject a callable[3]. The createForFormat() method takes that callable, calls it, and uses its return value as the actual encoder for the given format.

This fully dynamic and extensible implementation allows developers to add as many format-specific encoders as they want. Listing 2-11 shows what injecting the format-specific encoders looks like.

Listing 2-11. Dynamic Definition of Encoder Factories

```
$encoderFactory = new EncoderFactory();

$encoderFactory->addEncoderFactory(
    'xml',
    function () {
        return new XmlEncoder();
    }
);

$encoderFactory->addEncoderFactory(
    'json',
    function () {
        return new JsonEncoder();
    }
);

$genericEncoder = new GenericEncoder($encoderFactory);

$data = ...;

$jsonEncodedData = $genericEncoder->encode($data, 'json');
```

---

[3]See also the documentation for PHP's "callable" type: https://secure.php.net/manual/en/ language.types.callable.php

By introducing callable factories, we have relieved the `EncoderFactory` from the responsibility of providing the right constructor arguments for each encoder. In other words, we pushed knowledge about *creation logic* outside of the `EncoderFactory`, which makes it at once adhere to both the *Single Responsibility* principle and the *Open/Closed* principle.

PREFER IMMUTABLE SERVICES

As you may have noticed, `EncoderFactory` suddenly became a *mutable* service when we add the `addEncoderFactory()` method to it. This was a convenient thing to do, but in practice it'll be a smart to design a service to be *immutable*. Apply the following rule to achieve this:

After instantiation, it shouldn't be possible to change any of a service's properties.

The biggest advantage of a service being immutable is that its behavior won't change on subsequent calls. It will be fully configured before its first usage. And it will be impossible to somehow get different results upon subsequent calls.

If you still prefer having separate methods to configure an object, make sure to not make these methods part of the published interface for the class. They are there only for clients that need to configure the object, not for clients actually using the objects. For example, a dependency injection container will call `addEncoderFactory()` while setting up a new instance of `EncoderFactory`, but regular clients, like `GenericEncoder` itself, will only call `createForFormat()`.

Refactoring: Polymorphism

We have put some effort into implementing a nice abstract factory for encoders, but the `GenericEncoder` class still has this ugly `switch` statement for preparing the data before it is encoded (see Listing 2-12).

Listing 2-12. Revisiting prepareData()

```
class GenericEncoder
{
    private function prepareData($data, string $format)
    {
        switch ($format) {
            case 'json':
                $data = $this->forceArray($data);
                $data = $this->fixKeys($data);
                // fall through
            case 'xml':
                $data = $this->fixAttributes($data);
                break;
            default:
                throw new InvalidArgumentException(
                    'Format not supported'
                );
        }

        return $data;
    }
}
```

Where should we put this format-specific data preparation logic? In other words, whose *responsibility* would it be to prepare data before encoding it? Is it something the GenericEncoder should do? No, because preparing the data is format-specific, not generic. Is it the EncoderFactory? No, because it only knows about creating encoders. Is it one of the format-specific encoders? Yes! They know everything about encoding data to their own format.

So let's delegate the "prepare data" logic to the specific encoders by adding a method called prepareData($data) to the EncoderInterface and calling it in the encodeToFormat() method of the GenericEncoder (see Listing 2-13).

25

Listing 2-13. Moving prepareData() to EncoderInterface

```
interface EncoderInterface
{
    public function encode($data);

    /**
     * Do anything that is required to prepare the data for
     * encoding it.
     *
     * @param mixed $data
     * @return mixed
     */
    public function prepareData($data);
}

class GenericEncoder
{
    public function encodeToFormat($data, string $format): string
    {
        $encoder = $this->encoderFactory
                        ->createForFormat($format);

        /*
         * Preparing the data is now a responsibility of the
         * format-specific encoder
         */
        $data = $encoder->prepareData($data);

        return $encoder->encode($data);
    }
}
```

In the case of the JsonEncoder class, this would look like Listing 2-14.

Listing 2-14. An Example of a prepareData() Implementation

```
class JsonEncoder implements EncoderInterface
{
    public function encode($data): string
    {
        // ...
    }

    public function prepareData($data)
    {
        $data = $this->forceArray($data);
        $data = $this->fixKeys($data);

        return $data;
    }
}
```

This is not a great solution, because it introduces something called "temporal coupling": before calling encode() you always have to call prepareData(). If you don't, your data may be invalid and not ready to be encoded.

So instead, we should make *preparing* the data part of the *actual encoding* process inside the format-specific encoder. Each encoder should decide for itself if and how it needs to prepare the provided data before encoding it. Listing 2-15 shows what this looks like for the JSON encoder.

Listing 2-15. Making the Preparation of the Data Part of the encode() Method

```
class JsonEncoder implements EncoderInterface
{
    public function encode($data): string
    {
        $data = $this->prepareData($data);

        return json_encode($data);
    }
```

```
    private function prepareData($data)
    {
        // ...

        return $data;
    }
}
```

In this scenario, the `prepareData()` method is a private method. It is not part of the public interface of format-specific encoders, because it will only be used internally. The `GenericEncoder` is not supposed to call it anymore. We only have to remove it from the `EncoderInterface`, which now exposes a very clean API (see Listing 2-16).

Listing 2-16. The EncoderInterface

```
interface EncoderInterface
{
    public function encode($data): string;
}
```

Summarizing, the `GenericEncoder` we started with at the beginning of this chapter was quite specific. Everything was hard-coded, so it was impossible to change its behavior without modifying it. We first moved out the responsibility of creating the format-specific encoders to an encoder factory. Next we applied a bit of dependency inversion by introducing an interface for the encoder factory. Finally, we made the encoder factory completely dynamic: we allowed new format-specific encoder factories to be injected from the outside, i.e., without modifying the code of the encoder factory itself.

By doing all this, we made `GenericEncoder` *actually* generic. When we want to add support for another format we don't need to modify its code anymore. We only need to inject another callable in the encoder factory. This makes both classes (`GenericEncoder` and `EncoderFactory`) *open for extension* and *closed for modification*. In fact, maybe there is no longer a need for a `GenericEncoder` class anymore, if you consider what it looks like now (see Listing 2-17). We might ask users to directly call the encoder factory themselves.

Listing 2-17. The GenericEncoder May No Longer Deserve to be a Class

```
class GenericEncoder
{
    public function encodeToFormat($data, string $format): string
    {
        return $this->encoderFactory
                    ->createForFormat($format)
                    ->encode($data);
    }
}
```

Packages and the Open/Closed Principle

Applying the *Open/Closed* principle to classes in your project will greatly benefit the implementation of future requirements (or changed requirements) for that project. When the behavior of a class can be changed from the outside, without modifying its code, people will feel safe to do so. They won't need to be afraid that they will break something. They won't even need to modify existing unit tests for the class.

When it comes to packages, the *Open/Closed* principle is important for another reason. A package will be used in many different projects and in many different circumstances. This means that the classes in a package should not be too specific and leave room for the details to be implemented in different ways. And when behavior *has* to be specific (at some point a package has to be opinionated about something), it should be possible to change that behavior without actually modifying the code. Especially since most of the time that code cannot be changed by its users without cloning and maintaining the entire package themselves.

This is why the *Open/Closed* principle is highly useful and should be applied widely and generously when you are designing classes that are bound to end up in a reusable package. In practice, this means you allow classes to be configured by injecting different constructor arguments (also known as *dependency injection*). For collaborating objects that you may have extracted while applying the *Single Responsibility* principle, make sure these objects have a published interface, which allows users to decorate existing classes.

Applying the *Open/Closed* principle everywhere will make it possible to change the behavior of any class in your package by switching out or decorating constructor arguments only. Since users should never have to rely on subclassing to override a class's behavior anymore, this gives you the powerful option to mark all of them as final[4]. If you do this, you make it impossible for users to create subclasses for them. This decreases the number of possible use cases you need to consider when you make a change to the class. Effectively it will help you keep backward compatibility in the future, and give you all the freedom to change any implementation detail of the class.

Conclusion

Usually, if you want to change the behavior of a class, you'd need to modify its code. To prevent a class from being modified, in particular if that class is part of a package, you should build in options for changing the behavior of a class *from the outside*. In other words, it should be possible to extend its behavior without modifying any part of its code.

This is what it means to apply the *Open/Closed* principle: we make sure that objects are open for extension, but closed for modification. Several techniques to accomplish this have been discussed:

- Apply the *Single Responsibility* principle and extract collaborating objects.

- Inject collaborating objects as constructor arguments (*dependency injection*).

- Provide *interfaces* for collaborating objects, thereby allowing the user to replace dependencies, or *decorate* them.

- Mark classes as final, to make it impossible for the user to change the behavior of a class by extending it.

---

[4]An excellent discussion on the topic of marking classes as "final" can be found at:
Marco Pivetta, "When to Declare Classes Final," `https://ocramius.github.io/blog/when-to-declare-classes-final/`.

CHAPTER 3

The Liskov Substitution Principle

The *Liskov Substitution* principle can be stated as[1]:

> *Derived classes must be substitutable for their base classes.*

The funny thing about this principle is that it has the name of a person in it: Liskov. This is because the principle was first stated (using different wording) by Barbara Liskov. But otherwise, there are no surprises here; no big conceptual leaps. It seems only logical that derived classes, or "subclasses" as they are usually called, should be substitutable for their base, or "parent" classes. But of course there's more to it. This principle is not just a statement of the obvious.

Dissecting the principle, we recognize two conceptual parts. First it's about derived classes and base classes. Then it's about being substitutable.

The good thing is, we already know from experience what a *derived class* is: it's a class that extends some other class: the *base class*. Depending on the programming language you work with, a base class can be a concrete class, an abstract class, or an interface. If the base class is a *concrete class*, it has no "missing" (also known as *virtual*) methods. In this case a derived class, or subclass, overrides one or more of the methods that are already implemented in the parent class. On the other hand, if the base class is an *abstract class*, there are one or more *pure virtual methods* that have to be implemented by the derived class. Finally, if *all* of the methods of a base class are pure virtual methods (i.e., they only have a signature and no body), then generally the base class is called an *interface*.

---

[1]Robert C. Martin, "Principles of OOD," http://butunclebob.com/ArticleS.UncleBob. PrinciplesOfOod

© Matthias Noback 2018
M. Noback, *Principles of Package Design*, https://doi.org/10.1007/978-1-4842-4119-6_3

To make sure we're not lost in translation, take a look at Listing 3-1 for an explanation of the terms *base class*, *derived class,* and *interface* using PHP code.

Listing 3-1. The Differences Between an Interface, an Abstract Class, and a Regular Class

```php
/**
 * A concrete class: all methods are implemented, but can be
 * overridden by derived classes
 */
class ConcreteClass
{
    public function implementedMethod()
    {
        // ...
    }
}

/**
 * An abstract class: some methods need to be implemented by
 * derived classes
 */
abstract class AbstractClass
{
    abstract public function abstractMethod();

    public function implementedMethod()
    {
        // ...
    }
}

/**
 * An interface: all methods need to be implemented by derived
 * classes
 */
```

```
interface AnInterface
{
    public function abstractMethod();
}
```

Now we know all about base classes and derived classes. But what does it mean for derived classes to be *substitutable*? There is plenty of room for discussion it seems. In general, being substitutable is about *behaving well* as a subclass or a class implementing an interface. "Behaving well" would then mean behaving "as expected" or "as agreed upon".

Bringing the two concepts together, the *Liskov Substitution* principle says that if we create a class that extends another class or implements an interface, it has to behave as expected.

Words like "behaving as expected" are still pretty vague though. This is why pointing out violations of the *Liskov Substitution* principle can be pretty hard. Among developers, there may even be disagreement about whether or not something counts as a violation of the principle. Sometimes it's a matter of taste. And sometimes it depends on the programming language itself and the constructs it offers for object-oriented programming.

Nevertheless, we can point out some general bad practices that can prevent classes from being good substitutes for their parent classes or from being good implementations of an interface. So even though the principle itself is stated in a positive way, what follows is a discussion of some recurring violations of the principle. This will give you an idea of what it means to behave *badly* as a substitute for a class or an interface. This will indirectly help you to form an idea about how to behave *well* as a derived class.

Violation: A Derived Class Does Not Have an Implementation for All Methods

When a class does not have a proper implementation for all the methods of its parent class (or its interface for that matter), this results in a clear violation of the *Liskov Substitution* principle. It is bad behavior of substitutes to not do everything they are *supposed* to do. Consider for instance this `FileInterface` interface (see Listing 3-2).

Listing 3-2. The FileInterface

```
interface FileInterface
{
    public function rename(string $name): void;

    public function changeOwner(string $user, string $group): void;
}
```

It may seem obvious that a file always has a name and an owner and that both can be changed. But you may also imagine that for some files, changing the owner would not be possible at all. Take for instance files that are stored using a cloud storage provider like Dropbox. If we create a Dropbox implementation of the `FileInterface`, we have to prevent users from trying to change the owner of a file because that simply doesn't work for a Dropbox file (see Listing 3-3).

Listing 3-3. A Dropbox-Specific Implementation of FileInterface

```
class DropboxFile implements FileInterface
{
    public function rename(string $name): void
    {
        // ...
    }

    public function changeOwner(string $user, string $group): void
    {
        throw new BadMethodCallException(
            'Not implemented for Dropbox files'
        );
    }
}
```

Throwing exceptions like this should be considered bad behavior for substitutes: when someone calls the `changeOwner()` method of `DropboxFile`, their entire application might crash, without any warning.

In fact, we don't want a user to call `FileInterface::changeOwner()` when the class they use is `DropboxFile`. So maybe we can ask the user to check that, using a simple conditional (see Listing 3-4).

Listing 3-4. Using a Conditional to Check if We Can Change the File Owner

```
if (!$file instanceof DropboxFile) {
    $file->changeOwner(...);
}
```

This will prevent the nasty exception inside `changeOwner()` from being thrown. Unfortunately, this is not a viable solution. Most likely these lines will be repeated all over the user's codebase, quickly becoming a maintenance burden for them.

Instead of throwing an exception, we might just be secretive about the fact that you can't change the owner of a `DropboxFile` (see Listing 3-5).

Listing 3-5. Silently Skip Non-Implemented Methods

```
class DropboxFile implements FileInterface
{
    // ...

    public function changeOwner(string $user, string $group): void
    {
        // shhh... this is not supported, but who needs to know?
    }
}
```

Implementing this simple solution might be very tempting. Unfortunately, we can't do this—changing the owner of a file is a *significant operation*. It's about security after all. Some other parts of the system may count on `DropboxFile::changeOwner()` to *really* change the owner of the file; for instance, to make it unavailable for a previous owner. If for some reason changing the owner is not possible for a given type of file, it should be clear by its contract. In other words, its interface should not offer a method that makes it *seem* like this is possible.

The best solution would be to split the interface (see Listing 3-6).

Listing 3-6. Splitting FileInterface

```
interface FileInterface
{
    public function rename(string $name): void;
}
```

35

```
interface FileWithOwnerInterface extends FileInterface
{
    public function changeOwner(
        string $user,
        string $group
    ): void;
}
```

Together these interfaces form a hierarchy of file types. There is the generic file type defined by FileInterface (which only offers a method for it to be renamed). Then there is a subtype of files of which the owner can be changed. When we have defined these interfaces, the DropboxFile class would implement only the generic FileInterface interface (see Listing 3-7).

Listing 3-7. DropboxFile Doesn't Have to Implement changeOwner() Anymore

```
class DropboxFile implements FileInterface
{
    public function rename($name)
    {
        // ...
    }
}
```

And any other file type that supports a change of ownership, like LocalFile, implements FileWithOwnerInterface (see Listing 3-8).

Listing 3-8. LocalFile Implements Both rename() and changeOwner()

```
class LocalFile implements FileWithOwnerInterface
{
    public function rename(string $name): void
    {
        // ...
    }
```

```
public function changeOwner(string $user, string $group): void
{
    // ...
}
}
```

Figure 3-1 shows the resulting class hierarchy.

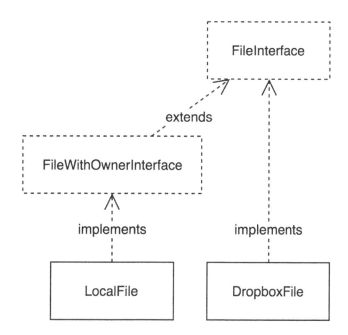

Figure 3-1. *The new hierarchy of file classes*

Finally we made the code adhere to the *Liskov Substitution* principle again. All the derived classes (DropboxFile and LocalFile) now behave well as substitutes for their base classes (FileInterface and FileWithOwnerInterface), and all of the methods of the base classes are properly implemented in the derived classes.

Leaky Abstractions

When we started out with this example, FileInterface was intended to be an abstraction for all the files in the world. The idea of a FileInterface was to expose some actions ("rename" or "change owner") that would work for any file, no matter where it's stored.

By trying to abstract (i.e., take away the details of) particular files and their behaviors, we made the incorrect assumption that *any* implementation of `FileInterface` would be able to provide meaningful implementations for *all* the methods of that interface.

When we started implementing `FileInterface` for a file stored with Dropbox, however, the assumption turned out to be wrong. `FileInterface` turned out to be an improper generalization of the "file" concept. Such an improper generalization is usually called a *leaky abstraction*. This term has been made famous by Joel Spolsky[2] when he stated his *Law of Leaky Abstractions*:

> *All non-trivial abstractions, to some degree, are leaky.*

As programmers, we are looking for *abstractions* all day. We want to treat a specific thing as a more general thing. When we do this consistently, we can later fearlessly replace any specific thing with some other specific thing. The system will not break because every part of it depends only on abstract things and doesn't care about the specifics.

The problem with most (all?) abstractions, as the *Law of Leaky Abstractions* states, is that they are *leaky*, which means that it will never be possible to abstract away every underlying specificness. Some underlying detail is bound to pop up and get in our way.

As long as you're aware of this limitation, though, you can still have a good time designing abstract things, which are only abstract up to a certain point. Just make sure the abstraction serves your purpose, and don't try to fit every possible specific thing in the world into your abstraction. This advice is known among scientists (and domain-driven design enthusiasts) as:

> *Essentially, all models are wrong, but some are useful.*[3]

Violation: Different Substitutes Return Things of Different Types

This violation applies in particular to programming languages that are not strictly typed, like PHP. These languages allow for a lot of uncertainty with regard to the type of, for instance, return values.

---

[2]Joel Spolsky, "The Law of Leaky Abstractions," `https://www.joelonsoftware.com/2002/11/11/the-law-of-leaky-abstractions/`

[3]Box, G. E. P.; Draper, N. R. (1987), *Empirical Model-Building and Response Surfaces*, John Wiley & Sons.

If a programming language has no way to pin down the type of the return value of a method, a common solution is to mention it inside the docblock of the method (see Listing 3-9).

Listing 3-9. The RouterInterface Interface

```
interface RouterInterface
{
    /**
     * @return Route[]
     */
    public function getRoutes();

    // ...
}
```

The getRoutes() method is supposed to return something iterable (hence the [ ]) containing Route objects. But different router implementations may return different types of iterable things, like arrays or (in PHP) an object that implements Traversable[4]. For instance, the SimpleRouter returns a plain array of Route objects (see Listing 3-10).

Listing 3-10. An Implementation of getRoutes() That Returns an Array

```
class SimpleRouter implements RouterInterface
{
    public function getRoutes()
    {
        $routes = [];

        // add Route objects to $routes
        $routes[] = ...;

        return $routes;
    }
}
```

---

[4]See the documentation for PHP's Traversable type at: https://secure.php.net/traversable

But the AdvancedRouter returns a much more advanced RouteCollection object (see Listing 3-11), which implements Traversable (actually, it implements Iterator[5], which itself implements Traversable).

Listing 3-11. An Implementation of getRoutes()That Returns a RouteCollection

```php
class AdvancedRouter implements RouterInterface
{
    public function getRoutes()
    {
        $routeCollection = new RouteCollection();

        // ...

        return $routeCollection;
    }
}

class RouteCollection implements Iterator
{
    // ...
}
```

Now AdvancedRouter and SimpleRouter look like good substitutes for RouterInterface, but in reality they are not. Even though both classes implement the getRoutes()method, they both return a value of a different type.

This violation of the *Liskov Substitution* principle may go unnoticed for a while, when people only iterate over the return value of getRoutes() using a simple foreach loop (see Listing 3-12).

Listing 3-12. Looping Over the Return Value of getRoutes()

```php
// $router implements RouterInterface, so $routes is iterable
$routes = $router->getRoutes();

foreach ($routes as $route) {
    // $route is a Route object
}
```

---

[5]See the documentation for PHP's Iterator type at: https://secure.php.net/iterator

This is bound to work in all situations, because `foreach` loops over the values in an array as well as over the values provided by an iterator. But since many things that are iterable (or at least all arrays) are also countable, one day someone may try to use the `count()` function on the return value of `getRoutes()` (see Listing 3-13).

Listing 3-13. Counting the Return Value of getRoutes()

```
if (count($routes) > 10) {
    // ...
}
```

Using the `SimpleRouter` this will work, but using the `AdvancedRouter` this won't work, since the `RouteCollection` does not implement `Countable`[6]. So it becomes clear that there is a problem with the relation between parent classes and their derived classes.

Contrary to the previous violation that we discussed, the problem is not that `SimpleRouter` and `AdvancedRouter` are bad substitutes for `RouterInterface`. The real problem is the ambiguously defined return type of its `getRoutes()` method: `Route[]`.

The solution to the problem is to define the type of the return value more strictly and to not allow for accidental deviations from the expected type. So interfaces and abstract classes should always document their return values in a strict way, using specific types[7] (Listing 3-14 shows an example of this).

Listing 3-14. Documenting Return Types

```
/**
 * @return array<Route>
 */
```

However, when we use the `array` type, this still leaves room for some questions. Arrays are pretty vague data structures. The implementer of this interface might wonder what type of keys they should use: integers or strings. And what are the expected values for those?

---

[6]See the documentation for PHP's `Countable` type at: `https://secure.php.net/countable`

[7]See the unofficial guideline for documenting types in PHP code, as proposed by phpDocumentor, at: `https://docs.phpdoc.org/references/phpdoc/types.html`

Because we still have this ambiguity, preferably we would introduce a new type to make sure that there can be no doubt. For example, we could define a RouteCollectionInterface interface to provide a contract for the return type of the getRoutes() method (see Listing 3-15).

Listing 3-15. Introducing the RouteCollectionInterface Interface

```
interface RouterInterface
{
    public function getRoutes(): RouteCollectionInterface;
}

interface RouteCollectionInterface extends Iterator, Countable
{
}
```

With the introduction of this new interface for collections of routes, it will be much easier for the derived classes (i.e., SimpleRouter and AdvancedRouter) to behave well as substitutes for their base class (i.e., RouterInterface). Now it's clear what their getRoutes() method is supposed to return.

Figure 3-2 shows what the class hierarchy looks like after the latest changes.

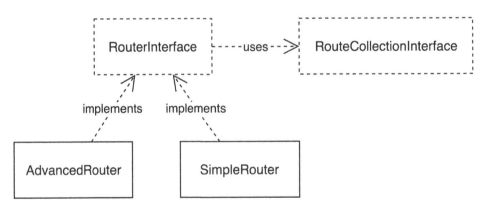

Figure 3-2. *The new dependency diagram*

More Specific Return Types Are Allowed

The *Liskov Substitution* principle does not allow for wrong or unspecific return types. Still, derived classes are allowed to return values that are *a subtype* of the type prescribed by the base class.

Consider the return type RouteCollectionInterface—any value that is an object that implements this interface will suffice as a proper return value, like an instance of SomeSpecificRouteCollectionClass (see Listing 3-16).

Listing 3-16. SomeSpecificRouteCollectionClass

```
class SomeSpecificRouteCollectionClass
    implements RouteCollectionInterface
{
    // ...
}
```

Any route collection class is a derived class of RouteCollectionInterface, hence, it's allowed as a return value. But the same goes for any class that *extends* such a route collection class, because the extending class is also supposed to be a well-behaving substitute for RouteCollectionInterface.

Violation: A Derived Class Is Less Permissive with Regard to Method Arguments

As we saw earlier, to be a good substitute means to implement all the required methods and make them return the right things, according to the contract of the base class. When it comes to method arguments, a substitute needs to be *equally or more permissive* than the contract defines.

What does it mean for a method to be "more or less permissive" about its method arguments? Well, let's take a look at a so-called "mass mailer". Its interface says it should have a single method: sendMail() (see Listing 3-17).

Listing 3-17. The MassMailerInterface Interface

```
interface MassMailerInterface
{
    public function sendMail(
        TransportInterface $ransport,
        Message $message,
        Recipients $recipients
    ): void;
}
```

Derived classes of this interface (i.e., base classes) should use the provided mail transport to send a message to all recipients at once. `TransportInterface` hides the messy details of how the message should be physically sent to the recipients. For instance, there may be implementations of `TransportInterface` that use `sendmail`, SMTP, or PHP's built-in `mail()` function to deliver mails.

Listing 3-18 is a partial implementation of the `MassMailerInterface`, which uses SMTP to send an email to lots of recipients at once. The first thing it does is verify that the user has provided the right type of argument for `$transport` (after all, this class only works with SMTP, so it needs an SMTP transport).

Listing 3-18. The SmtpMassMailer Implementation of MassMailerInterface

```
class SmtpMassMailer implements MassMailerInterface
{
    public function sendMail(
        TransportInterface $transport,
        Message $message,
        Recipients $recipients
    ): void {
        if (!($transport instanceof SmtpTransport)) {
            throw new InvalidArgumentException(
                'SmtpMassMailer only works with SMTP'
            );
        }
```

```
    // ...
  }
}
```

By restricting the set of allowed arguments—from all instances of TransportInterface to only instances of SmtpTransport—the SmtpMassMailer violates the *Liskov Substitution* principle. As a substitute of the base class MassMailerInterface, it's supposed to work with *any* mail transport, as long as it's an object of type TransportInterface. Instead, SmtpMassMailer is *less permissive* with regard to method arguments than the base class. This is *bad substitute behavior*.

The only way to fix this is to make sure that the contract of the base class reflects the needs of derived classes in a better way. Apparently, TransportInterface as a type for $transport is not sufficiently specific because it turns out that not every kind of mail transport is suitable for mass mailing.

Whenever we reason about class design like this, we need to keep an eye on phrases like:

> *not every ... is a ...*
>
> *not every ... can be used as a ...*

They usually indicate that there is something wrong with the type hierarchy of our classes. In this particular situation, our base classes/interfaces need to reflect that there are different kinds of mail transports. Redefining our class hierarchy, we might define a generic TransportInterface and one specialized TransportWithMassMailSupportInterface that extends TransportInterface. SmtpTransport should then implement TransportWithMassMailSupportInterface and the other transports merely implement TransportInterface (see Listing 3-19 and Figure 3-3).

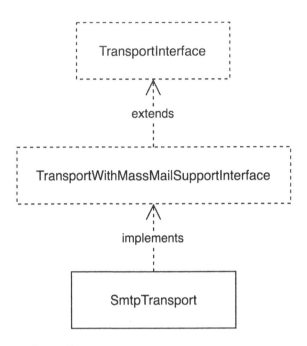

Figure 3-3. *The new class diagram*

Listing 3-19. Introducing a New Interface for Transports That Support Mass Mailing

```
class SmtpTransport implements
    TransportWithMassMailSupportInterface
{
    // ...
}
```

Finally we can change the expected type of the `$transport` argument to `TransportWithMassMailSupportInterface` to prevent the wrong type of transport from being provided to the `sendMail()` method (see Listing 3-20).

Listing 3-20. Using a More Specific Type for the Transport Parameter

```
interface MassMailerInterface
{
    public function sendMail(
        TransportWithMassMailSupportInterface $transport,
```

```
        Message $message,
        Recipients $recipients
    );
}
```

Then we can modify `SmtpMassMailer` and remove the extra check on the type of the provided `$transport` argument (see Listing 3-21).

Listing 3-21. There's No Need to Restrict Usage of sendMail() Anymore

```
class SmtpMassMailer implements MassMailerInterface
{
    public function sendMail(
        TransportWithMassMailSupportInterface $transport,
        Message $message,
        Recipients $recipients
    ): void {
        /*
         * No need to validate $transport anymore, it supports
         * mass mailing
         */

        // ...
    }
}
```

Finally, `SmtpMassMailer` adheres to the *Liskov Substitution* principle. It behaves well as a substitute because it does not put more restrictions on the input arguments than its base class (`MassMailerInterface`) does.

Depending on your particular situation, it may not be justifiable to introduce this extra layer of abstraction. Maybe you are trying to redefine things in an abstract way but they are really *just concrete things*. Or maybe you are trying to find similarities that can't be found because they don't exist. For example, it might be impossible to use any other transport for mass mailing than the SMTP transport. This means there can't be any other mass mailer than an SMTP mass mailer. Then we could just as well leave out the inappropriate abstraction called `MassMailerInterface` and define one concrete class suitable for mass mailing (see Listing 3-22).

Listing 3-22. Removing Abstraction Is an Option Too

```
class SmtpMassMailer
{
    public function sendMail(
        SmtpTransport $transport,
        Message $message,
        Recipients $recipients
    ): void {
        // ...
    }
}
```

Since `SmtpMassMailer` is not derived from a base class, it doesn't violate the *Liskov Substitution* principle anymore.

Violation: Secretly Programming Against a More Specific Type

Base classes like interfaces are used to expose an explicit public API. For instance, the public API of the `HttpKernelInterface` consists of just one method that is by definition public (see Listing 3-23).

Listing 3-23. The HttpKernelInterface Interface

```
interface HttpKernelInterface
{
    public function handle(Request $request): Response;
}
```

Sometimes derived classes have additional public methods. These methods constitute its *implicit* public API. The `getEnvironment()` method is an example of such a method (see Listing 3-24).

Listing 3-24. HttpKernel Adds Another Public Method: getEnvironment()

```
class HttpKernel implements HttpKernelInterface
{
    public function handle(Request $request): Response
    {
        // ...
    }

    public function getEnvironment(): string
    {
        // ...
    }
}
```

The getEnvironment() method is not defined in HttpKernelInterface. So whenever you want to use this method, you have to explicitly depend on the HttpKernel class, instead of the interface, like CachedHttpKernel does (see Listing 3-25). It wraps an HttpKernel instance and adds some additional HTTP caching functionality to it.

Listing 3-25. An Implementation of HttpKernelInterface: CachedHttpKernel

```
class CachedHttpKernel implements HttpKernelInterface
{
    public function __construct(HttpKernel $kernel)
    {
        if ($kernel->getEnvironment() === 'dev') {
            // ...
        }
    }

    public function handle(Request $request): Response
    {
        // ...
    }
}
```

As the creator of CachedHttpKernel, we might want to make it a bit more generic by allowing users to wrap *any* instance of HttpKernelInterface. This requires just a simple modification to the constructor of the class, as is done in Listing 3-26.

Listing 3-26. Calling getEnvironment() on an Instance of HttpKernelInterface

```
class CachedHttpKernel implements HttpKernelInterface
{
    public function __construct(HttpKernelInterface $kernel)
    {
        if ($kernel->getEnvironment() === 'dev') {
            // ...
        }
    }

    // ...
}
```

You may have spotted the problem already: we still use the getEnvironment() method, which was legitimate when the $kernel was guaranteed to be an instance of HttpKernel. After changing the type of the constructor argument, we can't be sure anymore. Now we only know that $kernel is an instance of HttpKernelInterface.

The provided argument might still be an instance of HttpKernel and since this is a PHP example, the code would run perfectly well in that case. The validity of the code is only determined at runtime, so even though the types don't match, we might still be able to call the getEnvironment() method on the $kernel.

So the CachedKernel pretends to be part of a nice hierarchy of substitutable classes, while in fact it isn't. It breaks the tradition of implementing and requiring just the handle() method of KernelInterface and thereby it violates the *Liskov Substitution* principle.

The solution to this problem is to be more careful about respecting the contracts of the base class. For example, we could expand the interface to contain the required getEnvironment() method (see Listing 3-27).

Listing 3-27. Adding getEnvironment() to KernelInterface

```
interface KernelInterface
{
    public function handle(Request $request): Response;

    public function getEnvironment(): string;
}
```

Or we could split the interface, just like we did on several previous occasions, so you can require more specific types of objects (see Listing 3-28).

Listing 3-28. Splitting the Interface

```
interface HttpKernelInterface
{
    public function handle(Request $request): Response;
}

interface HttpKernelWithEnvInterface
    extends HttpKernelInterface
{
    public function getEnvironment(): string;
}

class CachedHttpKernel implements HttpKernelInterface
{
    public function __construct(
        HttpKernelWithEnvironmentInterface $kernel
    ) {
        // ...
    }
}
```

As a last resort, you may verify that the actual argument implements the desired interface before calling its getEnvironment() method (as shown in Listing 3-29).

Listing 3-29. Checking for a Specific Type

```
class CachedHttpKernel implements HttpKernelInterface
{
    public function __construct(HttpKernelInterface $kernel)
    {
        if ($kernel instanceof HttpKernelWithEnvInterface) {
            $environment = $kernel->getEnvironment();
            // ...
        }
    }
}
```

Besides being an ad-hoc solution, it feels a lot like there is a missed opportunity for polymorphism here. We'd like to always be able to call getEnvironment() on an instance of HttpKernelInterface. So why not add it to the interface, thereby making sure that all implementations will return a sensible value when calling this method?

Packages and the Liskov Substitution Principle

The *Liskov Substitution* principle is relevant for you as a package developer in two ways: first, when your package defines an interface (or base class), and second, when your package provides an implementation of some interface (or base class), potentially one from a different package.

Defining an interface, as we've learned in the previous chapter, is useful when you want to provide a user with an extension point by means of *dependency injection* (and optionally *decoration*). If you provide a new interface, make sure it at least makes sense for a user to provide alternative implementations, which can still be proper substitutes for that interface. That is, get your abstractions right and don't force users to implement methods that don't make sense in *their* context. Sometimes this means you have to make an interface more narrow, offer multiple interfaces that can be implemented separately, or switch to a different level of abstraction. All cases will be covered in more detail in Chapter 4 when we discuss the *Interface Segregation* principle.

You can make it easier for implementers to write good substitutes for the interface you introduce by being specific about the types of arguments and return values. As we saw in the example about the getRoutes() method returning a

`RouteCollectionInterface` object, the situation can be drastically improved by introducing dedicated types. This is particularly true when the programming language's built-in types aren't useful or specific enough, or if it doesn't even support proper typing at all levels.

If your package contains a class that implements some interface, make sure this class adheres to the contract communicated by that interface and its accompanying documentation. In other words, make sure your implementation is a good substitute for the given interface ("base class"). This way, the user won't be confused when they switch implementations and things suddenly don't work anymore, or work in subtly different ways.

Finally, always consider the option *not to provide an interface* or base class for the user to implement or derive from. It may reduce the flexibility or extensibility of your package, but it will also make your package more *opinionated*. This often has the effect of making the package easier to understand and work with. Some things shouldn't be replaced by users; some things are just the way you want them to be, or how you think they make the most sense. It could be that the part that can't be reconfigured, replaced, or overridden by a user is also the part that makes your package stand out among the more generic ones.

Conclusion

The *Liskov Substitution* principle demands from derived classes that they are good substitutes. We discussed some examples of being a bad substitute. Based on these negative examples of bad substitutes, we can form an idea of what "being a good substitute" would mean. A good substitute:

- Provides an implementation for all the methods of the base class.

- Returns the type of things the base class prescribes (or more specific types).

- Doesn't put extra constraints on arguments for methods.

- Doesn't use non-strict typing to break the contract that was provided by the base class.

CHAPTER 4

The Interface Segregation Principle

The fourth SOLID principle is the *Interface Segregation* principle. It gives us the following instruction[1]:

> *Make fine-grained interfaces that are client specific.*

"Fine-grained interfaces" stands for interfaces with a small amount of methods. "Client specific" means that interfaces should define methods that make sense from the point of view of the client that *uses* the interface.

In order to reach an understanding of this principle, we will, just like in the previous chapter, discuss some common violations of it. Each violation is followed by a change in the code that would fix the problem.

Violation: Multiple Use Cases

Sometimes the interface of a class (i.e., its public API) contains too many methods because it serves multiple use cases. Some clients of the object will call a different set of methods than other clients of the same object.

Almost every existing *service container* implementation serves as a great example of a class that has different clients, since many service containers are used both as a dependency injection (or inversion of control) container *and* as a service locator.

A service container is an object you use to retrieve other objects (i.e., *services*), as demonstrated in Listing 4-1.

---

[1]Robert C. Martin, "The Principles of OOD," http://butunclebob.com/ArticleS.UncleBob. PrinciplesOfOod

© Matthias Noback 2018
M. Noback, *Principles of Package Design*, https://doi.org/10.1007/978-1-4842-4119-6_4

Listing 4-1. The ServiceContainerInterface

```
interface ServiceContainerInterface
{
    public function get(string $name);

    // ...
}

// $serviceContainer is an instance of ServiceContainerInterface
$mailer = $serviceContainer->get('mailer');
```

The `mailer` service will return a fully initialized object that can be used as a mailer. This allows for lazy loading of services. Because the service container locates services for you, a service container is also called a "service locator" (read more about why using a service locator is not a good idea in most cases in this article by Paul M. Jones[2]).

Before you can retrieve a service from a service container, some other part of the system should configure it correctly. The container should be instructed how to *initialize* services like the `mailer` service. This is the aspect of a service container that makes it a *dependency injection* container. See how this is done in Listing 4-2.

Listing 4-2. Configuring the Service Container Using set()

```
interface ServiceContainerInterface
{
    public function get(string $name);

    public function set(string $name, callable $factory): void;
}

// $serviceContainer is an instance of ServiceContainerInterface

// configure the mailer service
$serviceContainer->set(
    'mailer',
    function () use ($serviceContainer) {
```

---

[2]Paul M. Jones, "Quicker, Easier, More Seductive: Restraining Your Service Locators," http://paul-m-jones.com/archives/4792

```
        return new Mailer(
            // a mailer needs a transport
            $serviceContainer->get('mailer.transport')
        );
    }
);

// configure the mailer transport service
$serviceContainer->set(
    'mailer.transport',
    function () use ($serviceContainer) {
        return new MailerSmtpTransport();
    }
);
```

Other parts of the application don't need to worry anymore about how they should instantiate and initialize the `mailer` service—the creation logic is all handled by something else—the dependency injection container. This is why such a container is often called an *Inversion of Control (IoC) container*.

What's interesting is that the use case of *configuring* a service container (i.e., telling it how to instantiate services) is entirely different from the use case of fetching services from a service container (i.e., using it as a service locator). Still, both use cases will be provided by one and the same service container, since both `get()` and `set()` methods are defined in `ServiceContainerInterface`.

This means that any client that depends on `ServiceContainerInterface` can both *fetch* previously defined services and *define* new services. In reality, most clients of `ServiceContainerInterface` only perform one of these tasks. A client either configures the service container (for example, when the application is bootstrapped) *or* fetches a service from it (when the application is up and running).

When an interface tries to serve several types of clients at once, like the `ServiceContainerInterface` does, it violates the *Interface Segregation* principle. Such an interface is not fine-grained enough to be client-specific.

Refactoring: Separate Interfaces and Multiple Inheritance

One type of client is the part of the application that bootstraps the service container by configuring the available services. Such a client would only need the part of the ServiceContainerInterface that makes it mutable, i.e., its set() method. Another type of client is, for example, a controller that fetches a service to process a request. This type of client only needs get(), *not* set(). The difference between clients should be reflected in the interfaces that are available; for instance, by splitting the interface into a MutableServiceContainerInterface and a ServiceLocatorInterface, as is shown in Listing 4-3.

Listing 4-3. Splitting the Interface

```
interface MutableServiceContainerInterface
{
    public function set(string $name, callable $factory): void;
}

interface ServiceLocatorInterface
{
    public function get(string $name): object;
}
```

Now each client can require its own appropriate type of service container. In practice, there would be a single ServiceContainer class, which serves both types of clients at the same time by implementing both MutableServiceContainerInterface *and* ServiceLocatorInterface (see Listing 4-4 and Figure 4-1).

Listing 4-4. ServiceContainer Can Still Implement Both Interfaces

```
class ServiceContainer implements
    MutableServiceContainerInterface,
    ServiceLocatorInterface
{
    public function set(string $name, callable $factory): void
    {
```

```
        // ...
    }

    public function get(string $name): object
    {
        // ...
    }
}
```

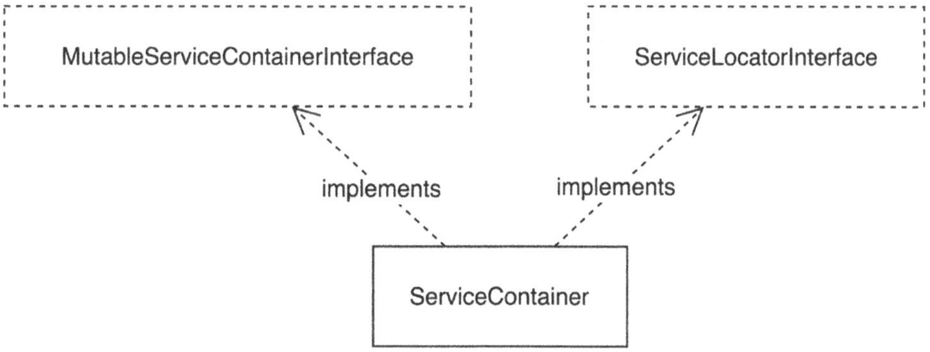

Figure 4-1. *The ServiceContainer class hierarchy*

None of the clients need to be bothered by this, since none of them will depend on the ServiceContainer class, only on one of the interfaces, as you can see in Listing 4-5.

Listing 4-5. Most Clients Will Depend on the ServiceLocatorInterface Only

```
class Kernel
{
    public function initializeServiceContainer(
        MutableServiceContainerInterface $serviceContainer
    ) {
        $serviceContainer->set(...);
    }
}
```

```php
class SomeController
{
    private $serviceLocator;

    public function __construct(
        ServiceLocatorInterface $serviceLocator
    ) {
        $this->serviceLocator = $serviceLocator;
    }

    public function indexAction(): Response
    {
        $mailer = $this->serviceLocator->get('mailer');

        // ...
    }
}
```

Having the ServiceContainer class implement both interfaces is not strictly necessary. It will just make it easier for you to maintain the code. The point to take from this is: it doesn't matter if a *class* does not strictly follow the *Interface Segregation* principle. That's not a problem, as long as all parts of the application depend only on one small, client-specific part of the public API of that class. To enable clients to do this, make sure that you always offer an interface. Then split that interface whenever you notice that different clients tend to use a different subset of its methods.

Violation: No Interface, Just a Class

Say you are working on a package called FabulousORM, which is supposed to contain a better object-relational mapper than any of the existing ones. You define an EntityManager class that can be used to persist entities (objects) in a relational database (see Listing 4-6). It uses a unit of work[3] to calculate the actual changes that need to be made to the database. The EntityManager class has some public methods—persist() and flush()—and one private method that internally makes the UnitOfWork object available to other methods.

---

[3]Martin Fowler, "Unit of Work," https://martinfowler.com/eaaCatalog/unitOfWork.html

Listing 4-6. The EntityManager Class

```
class EntityManager
{
    public function persist(object $entity): void
    {
        // ...
    }

    public function flush(): void
    {
        // ...
    }

    private function getUnitOfWork(): UnitOfWork
    {
        // ...
    }
}
```

People who use your package in their projects can depend on the EntityManager in their own classes, like the UserRepository does (see Listing 4-7).

Listing 4-7. The UserRepository Class

```
class UserRepository
{
    public function __construct(EntityManager $entityManager)
    {
        // ...
    }
}
```

Unfortunately, we can't use an interface as the type for the $entityManager constructor argument. The EntityManager class doesn't implement an interface. So the best we can do is use the class itself as the type for the constructor argument.

Even though there is no *explicit* interface for the EntityManager class, it still has an *implicit* interface. Each method of the class comes with a certain scope (public, protected, or private). When a client like UserRepository depends on the

EntityManager class, it depends on all the public methods of EntityManager: persist()
and flush(). None of the methods with a different scope (i.e., protected or private)
can be called by a client. So the public methods combined form the *implicit interface* of
EntityManager.

Implicit Changes in the Implicit Interface

One day you decide to add a Query class to your ORM package. It can be used to
query the database and retrieve entities from it. This Query class needs the UnitOfWork
object that is used internally by EntityManager. So you decide to turn its private
getUnitOfWork() method into a public method. That way, the Query class may depend
on the EntityManager class and use its getUnitOfWork(), as shown in Listing 4-8.

Listing 4-8. Query Needs EntityManager Only for Its UnitOfWork

```php
class EntityManager
{
    // ...

    /**
     * This method needs to be public because it's used by the
     * Query class
     */
    public function getUnitOfWork(): UnitOfWork
    {
        // ...
    }
}

class Query
{
    public function __construct(EntityManager $entityManager)
    {
        $this->entityManager = $entityManager;
    }
```

```
    public function someMethod()
    {
        $this->entityManager->getUnitOfWork()->...
    }
}
```

This new public method—getUnitOfWork()—will automatically become part of the *implicit interface* of EntityManager. From this moment on, all clients of EntityManager implicitly *depend* on this method too, even though they may only use the persist() and flush() methods.

This is a dangerous situation. Maybe some clients start using the publicly available method getUnitOfWork() too. They may do some pretty crazy things with the unit of work, which you would normally never authorize.

Adding methods to the implicit interface of a class is also bound to cause backward compatibility problems. Say that one day you refactor the Query class and remove its dependency on the EntityManager class. Since none of your classes need the public getUnitOfWork() method anymore, you then decide to make that method private again. Suddenly all the clients that use the previously public getUnitOfWork() method will break.

Refactoring: Add Header and Role Interfaces

You can solve this problem by defining an interface for each use case that the EntityManager class provides. For example, you may define the primary use case of "persisting entities" as the PersistsEntitiesInterface and introduce a second interface, HasUnitOfWorkInterface, to define a second use case (see Listing 4-9).

Listing 4-9. Use Header and Role Interfaces

```
interface PersistsEntitiesInterface
{
    public function persist(object $entity): void;

    public function flush(): void;
}
```

```
interface HasUnitOfWorkInterface
{
    public function getUnitOfWork(): UnitOfWork;
}
```

Then you can add a main interface that combines the two interfaces, and a class that implements the main interface (see Listing 4-10 and Figure 4-2).

Listing 4-10. The Header Interface for EntityManager Combines All Its Role Interfaces

```
interface EntityManagerInterface extends
    PersistsEntitiesInterface,
    HasUnitOfWorkInterface
{
}

class EntityManager implements EntityManagerInterface
{
    // ...
}
```

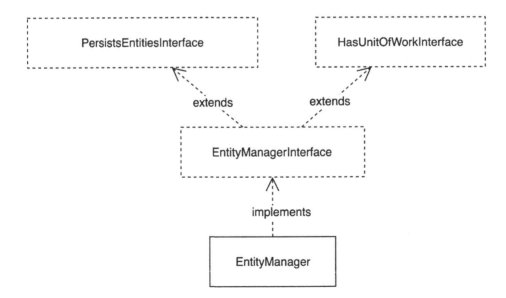

Figure 4-2. *The EntityManager class hierarchy*

Several of the interfaces we have just defined describe the *roles* that a class can play: `PersistsEntitiesInterface` and `HasUnitOfWorkInterface`. Then there is one interface that combines these roles and together constitutes a thing we know as an *entity manager*, which "can persist entities" and "has a unit of work": the `EntityManagerInterface`.

Martin Fowler calls these different types of interfaces role interfaces and header interfaces,[4] respectively. You can determine role interfaces for a class by looking at the different clients that use the class. Then you group the methods that are used together in separate interfaces, like we did for the `EntityManager` class.

Header interfaces are usually the easiest to define, since:

all you have to do is duplicate the public methods [of the class], no thought needed[5].

Often defining only a header interface is not enough, just like with the `EntityManager`. Clients won't need any other public methods than `persist()` and `flush()`. If the header interface could contain some other public methods, like `getUnitOfWork()`, they would be superfluous. As Robert C. Martin puts it[6]:

Clients should not be forced to depend on methods they do not use.

Packages and the Interface Segregation Principle

For package developers, applying the *Interface Segregation* principle has several advantages. First, it will lead to smaller interfaces, which are relevant for a subset of all the clients. As we saw earlier when discussing the *Single Responsibility* principle, making a class (or interface) smaller will reduce the number of reasons for it to change. An interface that needs to change less frequently is much preferable, since it will make it easier for you to maintain backward compatibility. An example would be the `ServiceLocatorInterface` we ended up with earlier in this chapter—having just a `get($id)` method makes the interface very stable and less likely to change.

Second, when you add a small, focused interface to a class in your package, you are free to add more public methods to that class that aren't part of the published interface.

[4]Martin Fowler, "RoleInterface," `https://martinfowler.com/bliki/RoleInterface.html`

[5]Martin Fowler, "RoleInterface," `https://martinfowler.com/bliki/RoleInterface.html`

[6]Robert C. Martin, "The Interface Segregation Principle," Engineering Notebook, C++ Report, Nov-Dec, 1996 (PDF available on `http://www.butunclebob.com/ArticleS.UncleBob. PrinciplesOfOod`).

You could even change or remove existing methods that aren't part of the interface, giving you more freedom to redesign or refactor classes without disturbing its users.

I'll repeat here that not every class in a package actually needs an interface. We'll take a moment to discuss some rules for when and when not to add an interface to a class at the end of Chapter 5.

Conclusion

An interface usually has multiple methods, although not every client of the interface uses the same subset of those methods. By depending on the interfaces, a client will be implicitly depending on all of the unused methods too. The *Interface Segregation* principle tells us to split (segregate) the interface methods according to how they are used.

Splitting an interface could happen by making a distinction between the particular roles of the larger interface. You will end up with a "header" interface and several "role" interfaces. Sometimes there is no overarching concept. In that case, segregating an interface will lead to several independent interfaces.

If a class has no explicit ("published") interface, the set of public methods it offers counts as its interface. To limit the number of public methods a client needs to depend on in order to use this class, you'd first need to publish an interface for the class. Then you can apply the *Interface Segregation* principle and make the interface smaller, or split it into separate ones for each set of clients.

## CHAPTER 5

The Dependency Inversion Principle

The last of the SOLID principles of class design focuses on class *dependencies*. It tells you what kinds of things a class should depend on[1]:

Depend on abstractions, not on concretions.

The name of this principle contains the word "inversion," from which we may infer that without following this principle we would usually depend on concretions, not on abstractions. The principle tells us to invert that direction: we should always depend on abstractions.

Example of Dependency Inversion: the FizzBuzz Generator

There is a well-known programming assignment that serves as a nice example of dependency inversion. It's called "FizzBuzz" and is often used as a little test to see if a candidate for a programming job could manage to implement a set of requirements, usually on the spot. The requirements are these:

- Generate a list of numbers from 1 to n.

- Numbers that are divisible by 3 should be replaced with Fizz.

- Numbers that are divisible by 5 should be replaced with Buzz.

- Numbers that are both divisible by 3 *and* by 5 should be replaced with FizzBuzz.

---

[1]Robert C. Martin, "The principles of OOD," http://butunclebob.com/ArticleS.UncleBob.PrinciplesOfOod

© Matthias Noback 2018
M. Noback, *Principles of Package Design*, https://doi.org/10.1007/978-1-4842-4119-6_5

Applying these rules, the resulting list would become:

> 1, 2, Fizz, 4, Buzz ... 13, 14, FizzBuzz, 16, 17 ...

Since not all the list's elements are integers, the resulting list should be a list of strings. A straightforward implementation might look like the one shown in Listing 5-1.

Listing 5-1. An Implementation of the FizzBuzz Algorithm

```
class FizzBuzz
{
    public function generateList(int $limit): array
    {
        $list = [];

        for ($number = 1; $number <= $limit; $number++) {
            $list[] = $this->generateElement($number);
        }

        return $list;
    }

    private function generateElement(int $number): string
    {
        if ($number % 3 === 0 && $number % 5 === 0) {
            return 'FizzBuzz';
        }

        if ($number % 3 === 0) {
            return 'Fizz';
        }

        if ($number % 5 === 0) {
            return 'Buzz';
        }

        return (string)$number;
    }
}

$fizzBuzz = new FizzBuz();
$list = $fizzBuzz->generateList(100);
```

Given the assignment, this is a very accurate implementation of the requirements. Reading through the code, we are able to recognize every requirement in it: the rules about the divisibility of the numbers, the requirement that the list of numbers starts at 1, etc.

Once the candidate has produced some code like this, the interviewer adds another requirement:

> It should be possible to add an extra rule *without modifying* the FizzBuzz class.

Making the FizzBuzz Class Open for Extension

Currently the FizzBuzz class is not open for extension, nor closed for modification. If numbers divisible by 7 should one day be replaced with Whizz, it will be impossible to implement this change without actually modifying the code of the FizzBuzz class.

Pondering about the design of the FizzBuzz class and how we can make it more flexible, we note that the generateElement() method contains lots of details. Within the same class, though, the generateList() method is rather generic. It just generates a list of incrementing numbers, starting with 1 (which is somewhat specific), and ending with a given number. So the FizzBuzz class has two responsibilities: it generates lists of numbers, and it replaces certain numbers with something else, based on the FizzBuzz rules.

These FizzBuzz rules are liable to change. And the requirement is that when the rules change, we should not need to modify the FizzBuzz class itself. So let's apply some things that we've learned in the chapter about the *Open/Closed* principle. For starters, we can extract the rules into their own classes and use them in generateElement(), as shown in Listing 5-2.

Listing 5-2. Extracting a Method for Generating Separate Elements Using "Rules"

```
class FizzBuzz
{
    public function generateList(int $limit): array
    {
        // ...
    }
```

```
    private function generateElement(int $number): string
    {
        $fizzBuzzRule = new FizzBuzzRule();
        if ($fizzBuzzRule->matches($number)) {
            return $fizzBuzzRule->getReplacement();
        }

        $fizzRule = new FizzRule();
        if ($fizzRule->matches($number)) {
            return $fizzRule->getReplacement();
        }

        $buzzRule = new BuzzRule();
        if ($buzzRule->matches($number)) {
            return $buzzRule->getReplacement();
        }

        return (string)$number;
    }
}
```

The details about the rules can be found in the specific rule classes. Listing 5-3 shows an example of the "Fizz" rule, as implemented in the FizzRule class.

Listing 5-3. A Class that Represents One of the FizzBuzz Rules

```
class FizzRule
{
    public function matches($number): bool
    {
        return $number % 3 === 0;
    }

    public function getReplacement(): string
    {
        return 'Fizz';
    }
}
```

This is one step in the right direction. Even though the details about the rules (the numbers 3, 5, 3 and 5, and their replacement values) have been moved to the specific rule classes, the code in generateElement() remains very specific. The rules are still represented by (very specific) class names, and adding a new rule would still require a modification of the generateElement() method, so we haven't exactly made the class *open for extension* yet.

Removing Specificness

We can remove this specificness from the FizzBuzz class by introducing an interface (see Listing 5-4) for the rule classes and allowing multiple rules to be injected into a FizzBuzz instance.

Listing 5-4. Introducing Abstraction

```
interface RuleInterface
{
    public function matches($number): bool;

    public function getReplacement(): string;
}

class FizzBuzz
{
    private $rules = [];

    public function addRule(RuleInterface $rule): void
    {
        $this->rules[] = $rule;
    }

    public function generateList($limit): array
    {
        // ...
    }
```

```
    private function generateElement(int $number): string
    {
        foreach ($this->rules as $rule) {
            if ($rule->matches($number)) {
                return $rule->getReplacement();
            }
        }

        return $number;
    }
}
```

Now we need to make sure that every specific rule class implements the RuleInterface and then the FizzBuzz class can be used to generate lists of numbers with varying rules, as shown in Listing 5-5 and Figure 5-1.

Listing 5-5. Setting Up a FizzBuzz Instance with Concrete Rules

```
class FizzRule implements RuleInterface
{
    // ...
}

$fizzBuzz = new FizzBuzz();
$fizzBuzz->addRule(new FizzBuzzRule());
$fizzBuzz->addRule(new FizzRule());
$fizzBuzz->addRule(new BuzzRule());
// add more rules if you want, e.g.
// $fizzBuzz->addRule(new WhizzRule());
// ...

$list = $fizzBuzz->generateList(100);
```

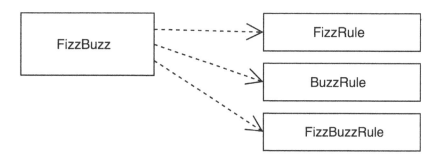

Figure 5-1. *FizzBuzz with concrete dependencies*

Now we have a highly generic piece of code, the `FizzBuzz` class, which "generates a list of numbers, replacing certain numbers with strings, based on a flexible set of rules". There's no mention of "FizzBuzz" in that description and there's no mention of "Fizz" nor "Buzz" in the code of the `FizzBuzz` class. Actually, the `FizzBuzz` class may be renamed so that it better communicates its responsibility. Of course, naming things is one of the hardest parts of our job and `NumberListGenerator` isn't a particularly expressive name, but it would better describe its purpose than its current name.

Looking at the initial implementation of the `FizzBuzz` class, it has become clear that the class had an abstract task from the start: to generate a list of numbers. Only the rules were highly detailed (being divisible by 3, by 5, etc.). To use the words from the *Dependency Inversion* principle: an abstraction depended on concrete things. This caused the `FizzBuzz` class to be closed for extension, as it was impossible to add another rule without modifying it.

By introducing the `RuleInterface` and adding specific rule classes that implemented this interface, we fixed the dependency direction. The `FizzBuzz` class started to depend on more abstract things, called "rules" (see Figure 5-2). When creating a new `FizzBuzz` instance, concrete implementations of `RuleInterface` have to be injected in the right order. This will result in the correct execution of the FizzBuzz algorithm. The `FizzBuzz` class itself is no longer concerned about it, which is why the class ends up being more flexible with regard to changing requirements. This is exactly the way things should be according to the *Dependency Inversion* principle[2]:

> *Abstractions should not depend upon details. Details should depend upon abstractions.*

[2]Robert C. Martin (May 1996), "The Dependency Inversion Principle," C++ Report (PDF available at `http://www.butunclebob.com/ArticleS.UncleBob.PrinciplesOfOod`).

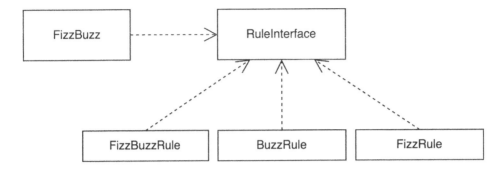

Figure 5-2. *FizzBuzz with abstract dependencies*

Now that we've seen the *Dependency Inversion* principle in action, we can take a look at some situations where it's clearly being violated.

Violation: A High-Level Class Depends on a Low-Level Class

The first violation arises from *mixing different levels of abstraction*. It's an interesting concept that needs further explanation before we dive into the example.

On a daily basis we have to deal with a great diversity of things that exist in the universe. We wouldn't be able to do anything meaningful if we'd consider every little detail of everything we talk about, everything we use while doing our job, everyone we love. So to preserve our sanity, we come up with abstractions all the time. "Abstraction" means "taking away the details". What remains is a concept that can we can use to *group* all the specific things from which the abstraction has been created, and a name for what's *essential* to all these specific things, ignoring the little differences.

In conversation we usually end up establishing some level of abstraction, so we can safely ignore the details (or the larger picture). When discussing software design, this means we zoom in or out until we can address the issue at hand. For instance, when discussing a code smell, we'll be talking about method signatures, variable names, etc. so we can safely ignore the message queue software, or the particular Linux filesystem that we use on our server. When we talk about how the application gets data from the database, we discuss SQL queries, so we can ignore the underlying TCP protocol that's being used.

Zooming in and out is the same as moving from abstraction to concretion and back again. The more we zoom in on a part of our software, the closer we get to the low-level details (also known as "internals"). The more we zoom out, the closer we get to a high-level view of the system; what features it aims to provide to its users.

In class design, we have to consider the same kind of zooming in and out. Every class has two levels of abstraction: the first is the one perceived by clients. The second is the one that's going on inside. By definition, a class or an interface is going to hide some implementation details for its client, meaning that the clients will perceive it to be more abstract, while the class internally is more concrete.

So a class's internals are always more concrete than the abstraction that the class represents. However, when a class depends on some other class, it should again depend on something that is abstract, not concrete. That way, the class itself becomes a client of something abstract and can safely ignore all the underlying details of how that dependency works under the hood.

As an example of a class that has a dependency that *isn't* abstract, consider the Authentication class in Listing 5-6.

Listing 5-6. The Authentication Class

```
class Authentication
{
    private $connection;

    public function __construct(Connection $connection)
    {
        $this->connection = $connection;
    }

    public function checkCredentials(
        string $username,
        string $password
    ): void {
        $user = $this->connection->fetchAssoc(
            'SELECT * FROM users WHERE username = ?',
            [$username]
        );
```

```
    if ($user === null) {
        throw new InvalidCredentialsException(
            'User not found'
        );
    }

    // validate password

  }
}
```

The Authentication class needs a database connection (see Figure 5-3), in this case represented by a Connection object. It uses the connection to retrieve the user data from the database.

Figure 5-3. *The Authentication class depends on Connection*

There are many problems with this approach. They can be articulated by answering the following questions about this class:

1. *Is it important for an authentication mechanism to deal with the exact location of the user data?*

    Well, definitely not. The only thing the Authentication class really needs is user data, as an array or preferably an object representing a user. The *origin* of that data is irrelevant.

2. *Is it possible to fetch user data from some other place than a database?*

    Currently it's impossible. The Authentication class requires a Connection object, which is a *database* connection. You can't use it to retrieve users from, for instance, a text file or from some external web service.

Looking at the answers, we have to conclude that both the *Single Responsibility* principle and the *Open/Closed* principle have been violated in this class. The Authentication class is not only concerned about the authentication mechanism itself, but also about the actual storage of the user data. Furthermore, it's impossible to reconfigure the class to look in a different place for user data. The underlying reason for these issues is that the *Dependency Inversion* principle has been violated too: the Authentication class itself is a *high-level abstraction*. Nevertheless, it depends on a very *low-level concretion*: the database connection. This particular dependency makes it impossible for the Authentication class to fetch user data from any other place than the database.

Trying to rephrase what the Authentication class really needs, we realize that it's not a database connection, but merely something that can *provide* the user data. Let's call that thing a "user provider". The Authentication class doesn't need to know anything about the actual process of fetching the user data (whether it originates from a database, a text file, or an LDAP server). It only needs the user data.

It's a good thing for the Authentication class not to care about the origin of the user data itself. All the implementation details about fetching user data can be left out of that class. At once, the class will become highly reusable, because it will be possible for users of the class to implement their own "user providers".

Refactoring: Abstractions and Concretions Both Depend on Abstractions

Refactoring the high-level Authentication class to make it follow the *Dependency Inversion* principle means we should first remove the dependency on the low-level Connection class. Then we add a higher-level dependency on something that provides the user data, the UserProvider class (see Listing 5-7).

Listing 5-7. Introducing the UserProvider Class

```
class Authentication
{
    private $userProvider;

    public function __construct(UserProvider $userProvider)
    {
        $this->userProvider = $userProvider;
    }
```

```php
    public function checkCredentials(
        string $username,
        string $password
    ): void {
        $user = $this->userProvider->findUser($username);

        if ($user === null) {
            throw new InvalidCredentialsException(
                'User not found'
            );
        }

        // validate password
    }
}

class UserProvider
{
    private $connection;

    public function __construct(Connection $connection)
    {
        $this->connection = $connection;
    }

    public function findUser(string $username): array
    {
        return $this->connection->fetchAssoc(
            'SELECT * FROM users WHERE username = ?',
            [$username]
        );
    }
}
```

The Authentication class has nothing to do with a database anymore (as depicted in Figure 5-4). Instead, the UserProvider class does everything that's needed to fetch a user from the database.

Figure 5-4. *Authentication depends on UserProvider*

It's still not easy to switch between different user provider implementations. The `Authentication` class depends on the concrete `UserProvider` class. If anybody wants to fetch their user data from a text file, they'd have to extend this class and override its `findUser()` method (as is done in Listing 5-8).

Listing 5-8. Overriding Functionality of UserProvider

```
class TextFileUserProvider extends UserProvider
{
    public function findUser(string $username): array
    {
        // ...
    }
}
```

They would thereby inherit any behavior that was implemented in the `UserProvider` class itself and that's not a desirable situation. The solution is to provide an interface, e.g. `UserProviderInterface`, for any class that wants to be a user provider. Then every class that implements this interface can and should also have a more meaningful name than `UserProvider`, e.g. `MySQLUserProvider` (see Listing 5-9).

Listing 5-9. Introducing the UserProviderInterface and Some Implementations

```
interface UserProviderInterface
{
    public function findUser(string $username): array;
}

class MySQLUserProvider implements UserProviderInterface
{
    // ...
}
```

```
class TextFileUserProvider implements UserProviderInterface
{
    // ...
}
```

And of course we have to change the type of the constructor argument of the Authentication class to UserProviderInterface (see Listing 5-10).

Listing 5-10. The Authentication Class Now Accepts a UserProviderInterface

```
class Authentication
{
    private $userProvider;

    public function __construct(
        UserProviderInterface $userProvider
    ) {
        $this->userProvider = $userProvider;
    }

    // ...
}
```

As you can see in the dependency diagram in Figure 5-5, the high-level class Authentication does not depend on low-level, concrete classes like Connection anymore. Instead, it depends on another high-level, abstract thing: UserProviderInterface. Both are conceptually on more or less the same level. Lower-level operations like reading from a file and fetching data from a database are performed by lower-level classes—the concrete user providers. This completely conforms to the *Dependency Inversion* principle, which states that:

> *High-level modules should not depend upon low-level modules. Both should depend upon abstractions.*[3]

---

[3]Robert C. Martin (May 1996), "The Dependency Inversion Principle," C++ Report (PDF available at http://www.butunclebob.com/ArticleS.UncleBob.PrinciplesOfOod).

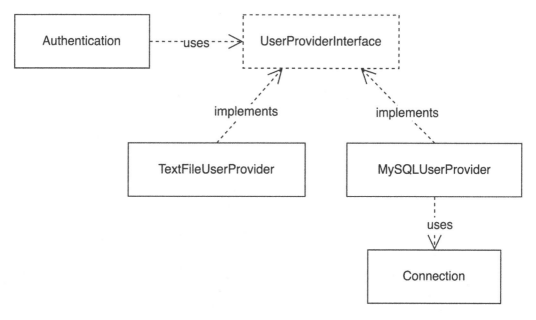

Figure 5-5. *Authentication depends on UserProviderInterface*

A nice side-effect of the changes we made is that the maintainability of the code has greatly improved. When a bug is found in one of the queries used for fetching user data from the database, there's no need to modify the Authentication class itself anymore. The necessary changes will only occur inside the specific user provider, in this case the MySQLUserProvider. This means that this refactoring has greatly reduced the chance that you will accidentally break the authentication mechanism itself.

SIMPLY DEPENDING ON AN INTERFACE IS NOT ENOUGH

The step from UserProvider to UserProviderInterface was an important one because it helped users of the Authentication class easily switch between user provider implementations. But just adding an interface to a class is not always sufficient to fix all problems related to dependencies.

Consider an alternative version of the UserProviderInterface, shown in Listing 5-11.

Listing 5-11. An Alternative UserProviderInterface

```
interface UserProviderInterface
{
    public function findUser(string $username): array;

    public function getTableName(): string;
}
```

This is not a helpful interface at all. It's an immediate violation of the *Liskov Substitution* principle. Not all classes that implement this interface will be able to be good substitutes for it. If one implementation doesn't use a database table for storing user data, it most certainly won't be able to return a sensible value when someone calls getTableName() on it. But more importantly: the UserProviderInterface mixes different levels of abstraction and combines something high-level like "finding a user" with something low-level like "the name of a database table".

So even if we would introduce this interface to make the Authentication class depend on an abstraction instead of concretion, that goal won't be reached. In fact, the Authentication class will still depend on something concrete and low-level: a user provider that is table-based.

Violation: Vendor Lock-In

In this section, we discuss a common violation of the *Dependency Inversion* principle that is especially relevant to package developers. Say a class needs some way to fire application-wide events. The usual solution for this is to use an event dispatcher (sometimes called "event manager"). The problem is that there are many event dispatchers available, and they all have a slightly different API. For instance, the Symfony EventDispatcherInterface[4] looks like the one in Listing 5-12.

---

[4]https://github.com/symfony/event-dispatcher/blob/2.3/EventDispatcherInterface.php

Listing 5-12. The EventDispatcherInterface

```
interface EventDispatcherInterface
{
    public function dispatch(
        string $eventName,
        Event $event = null
    ): void;

    public function addListener(
        string $eventName,
        callable $listener,
        int $priority = 0
    );

    // ...
}
```

Note that events are supposed to have a name, which is a string (e.g., `"new_user"`), and when firing (or "dispatching") the event you can provide an `Event` object carrying additional contextual data. The event object will be enriched and used as the first argument when the event listener (which can be any PHP callable) gets notified. An example of an event and an event listener class can be found in Listing 5-13.

Listing 5-13. An Event Class and an Event Listener

```
use Symfony\Component\EventDispatcher\Event;

class NewUserEvent extends Event
{
    private $user;

    public function __construct(User $user)
    {
        $this->user = $user;
    }
```

```php
    public function getUser(): User
    {
        return $this->user;
    }
}

class EventListener
{
    public function onNewUser(NewUserEvent $event): void
    {
        // ...
    }
}

$eventDispatcher = new EventDispatcher();
$eventDispatcher->addListener(
    'new_user',
    [new EventListener(), 'onNewUser']
);

$user = new User();
$eventDispatcher->dispatch('new_user', new NewUserEvent($user))
```

An event dispatcher from another framework, Laravel looks like the one in Listing 5-14 (based on version 4.0 of the framework[5]).

Listing 5-14. The Event Dispatcher from the Laravel Framework

```php
class Dispatcher
{
    public function listen(
        string $event,
        callable $listener,
        int $priority = 0
    ): void {
        ...
    }
```

---

[5]https://github.com/laravel/framework/blob/4.0/src/Illuminate/Events/Dispatcher.php

```
public function fire(string $event, array $payload = []): void
{
    // ...
}

// ...
}
```

Note that it doesn't implement an interface. And instead of an event object, the contextual data for events (the "payload") consist of an array, which will be used as a method argument when a listener gets notified of an event. See Listing 5-15 for an example of how it's used.

Listing 5-15. Using the Laravel Event Dispatcher

```
class EventListener
{
    public function onNewUser(User $user)
    {
        // ...
    }
}

$dispatcher = new Dispatcher();
$dispatcher->listen(
    'new_user',
    [new EventListener(), 'onNewUser']
);

$user = new User();
$dispatcher->fire('new_user', [$user]);
```

It appears that you can do more or less the same things with both event dispatchers, i.e. fire events and listen to them. But the way you do it is different in subtle ways.

Let's say the package you're working on contains a UserManager class like the one in Listing 5-16. Using this class you can create new users. Afterwards you want to dispatch an application-wide event, so other parts of the application can respond to the fact that a new user now exists (for instance, maybe new users should receive a welcome email).

Listing 5-16. The UserManager Class

```
use Illuminate\Events\Dispatcher;

class UserManager
{
    public function create(User $user): void
    {
        // persist the user data

        // ...

        // fire an event: "new_user"
    }
}
```

Let's assume you want to use the package containing the UserManager class in a Laravel application. Laravel already provides an instance of the Dispatcher class in its Inversion of Control (IoC) container. This means you can easily inject it as a constructor argument of the UserManager class, as is done in Listing 5-17.

Listing 5-17. Using the Laravel Event Dispatcher in the UserManager

```
use Illuminate\Events\Dispatcher;

class UserManager
{
    private $dispatcher;

    public function __construct(Dispatcher $dispatcher)
    {
        $this->dispatcher = $dispatcher;
    }

    public function create(User $user): void
    {
        // ...

        $this->dispatcher->fire('new_user', ['user' => $user]);
    }
}
```

A couple of weeks later, you start working on a project built with the Symfony framework. You want to reuse the UserManager class, since it offers exactly the functionality that you need, and you install the package containing it inside this new project. Now, a Symfony application also has an event dispatcher readily available in its service container. But this event dispatcher is an instance of EventDispatcherInterface. It's *impossible* to use the Symfony event dispatcher as a constructor argument for the UserManager class because the type of the argument wouldn't match the type of the injected service. You have effectively *prevented reuse* of the UserManager class.

If you still want to use the UserManager class in a Symfony project, you would need to add an extra dependency on the illuminate/events package to make the Laravel Dispatcher class available in your project. You'd have to configure a service for it, next to the already existing Symfony event dispatcher and end up having two global event dispatchers. Then you'd still need to bridge the gap between the two types of dispatchers, since events fired on the Laravel Dispatcher won't be fired automatically on the Symfony event dispatcher too. In fact, they even use incompatible types (event objects versus arrays).

The moment you picked the Laravel event dispatcher as the event dispatcher of your choice, you coupled the package to a specific implementation, making it harder or impossible to just use the package in a project that uses a different event dispatcher. Introducing such a dependency to your package is known as "vendor lock-in"; it will only work with third-party code from a specific vendor.

Solution: Add an Abstraction and Remove the Dependency Using Composition

As we discussed earlier, depending on a concrete class can be problematic all by itself because it makes it hard for users to switch between implementations of that dependency. Therefore, we should introduce our own interface, which decouples this class from any concrete event dispatcher implementation. This abstract event dispatcher is not framework-specific, it just offers one method that can be used to dispatch events. Then we can change the UserManager class to only accept an event dispatcher, which is an instance of our very own DispatcherInterface (see Listing 5-18).

Listing 5-18. Introducing an Abstraction and Using it in UserManager

```
interface DispatcherInterface
{
    public function dispatch($eventName, array $context = []);
}

class UserManager
{
    private $dispatcher;

    public function __construct(DispatcherInterface $dispatcher)
    {
        $this->dispatcher = $dispatcher;
    }

    // ...
}
```

The UserManager is now fully decoupled from the framework. It uses its own event dispatcher, which is quite generic and contains the least amount of details possible.

Of course, our DispatcherInterface is not a working event dispatcher itself. We need to bridge the gap between that interface and the concrete event dispatchers from Laravel and Symfony. We can do this using the *Adapter* pattern[6]. Using object composition, we can make the Laravel Dispatcher class compatible with our own DispatcherInterface, as shown in Listing 5-19.

Listing 5-19. Concrete Implementation of the Abstract DispatcherInterface That Uses the Laravel Event Dispatcher

```
use Illuminate\Events\Dispatcher;

class LaravelDispatcher implements DispatcherInterface
{
    private $dispatcher;

    public function __construct(Dispatcher $dispatcher)
```

---

[6]Erich Gamma e.a., *Design Patterns: Elements of Reusable Object-Oriented Software*, Addison-Wesley, 1994.

```
    {
        $this->dispatcher = $dispatcher;
    }

    public function dispatch(
        string $eventName,
        array $context = []
    ): void {
        $this->dispatcher->fire(
            $eventName,
            array_values($context)
        );
    }
}
```

By introducing the DispatcherInterface, we have cleared the way for users of other frameworks to implement their own adapter classes. These adapter classes only have to conform to the public API defined by our DispatcherInterface. Under the hood they can use their own specific type of event dispatcher. For example, the adapter for the Symfony event dispatcher would look like the one shown in Listing 5-20.

Listing 5-20. Alternative Implementation of DispatcherInterface That Uses the Symfony Event Dispatcher

```
use Symfony\Component\EventDispatcher\EventDispatcherInterface;
use Symfony\Component\EventDispatcher\GenericEvent;

class SymfonyDispatcher implements DispatcherInterface
{
    private $dispatcher;

    public function __construct(
        EventDispatcherInterface $dispatcher
    ) {
        $this->dispatcher = $dispatcher;
    }
```

```
public function dispatch(
    string $eventName,
    array $context = []
): void {
    $this->dispatcher->dispatch(
        $eventName,
        new GenericEvent(null, $context)
    );
}
}
```

Before we introduced the DispatcherInterface, the UserManager depended on something *concrete*—the Laravel-specific implementation of an event dispatcher, as depicted in Figure 5-6.

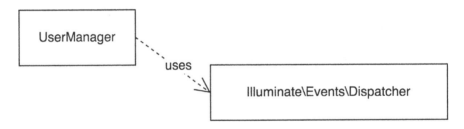

Figure 5-6. *The UserManager has a dependency on the concrete Laravel Dispatcher*

After we added the DispatcherInterface, the UserManager class now depends on something *abstract*. In other words, we inverted the dependency direction, which is exactly what the *Dependency Inversion* principle tells us to do. The resulting dependency diagram is shown in Figure 5-7.

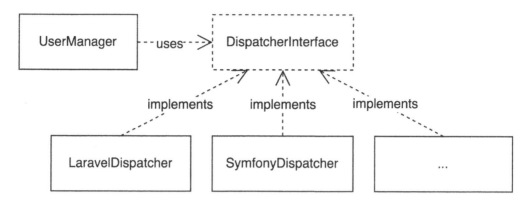

Figure 5-7. *The UserManager has a dependency on an abstract dispatcher, on which several adapters depend*

Packages and the Dependency Inversion Principle

Although the *Dependency Inversion* principle is a class design principle, it's all about the *relationship* between classes. This relationship often crosses the boundaries of a package. Therefore the *Dependency Inversion* principle resonates strongly at a package level. According to this principle, classes should depend on abstractions, not on concretions. In parallel to this, packages themselves should also depend in the direction of abstractness, as we see in Chapter 11.

Depending on Third-Party Code: Is It Always Bad?

We got rid of vendor lock-in for the UserManager class and we now know the principle by which we can achieve the same thing in many other situations. However, in doing so, there's a certain cost involved—the cost of defining our own interface and our own adapter implementations. Even if we use dependency inversion for every dependency of every class, there are still other ways in which our code will remain dependent on third-party code.

So the question is, in which cases should we allow ourselves to depend on third-party code and which cases definitely call for dependency inversion?

First, we need to make a distinction between frameworks and libraries. Even though both can be distributed as packages, the difference is most apparent if you consider how they deal with your code. Frameworks follow the *Hollywood* principle[7]: "Don't call

---

[7]Craig Larman, *Applying UML and Patterns*, Prentice Hall (2001).

us, we'll call you". For instance, a web server may forward an HTTP request to your web application, and its framework will analyze the request and call one of your controllers. Once the framework has called *your* code (also known as "userland code"), you're free to use anything to accomplish your task, including third-party library code. Figure 5-8 shows how framework, userland, and library code call each other.

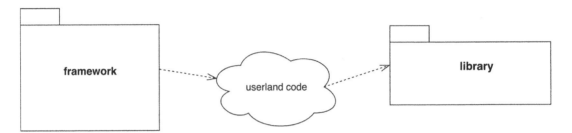

Figure 5-8. *Framework calls userland code, which calls library code*

If you're a package developer who wants to extract part of the userland code and publish it as a package, you should only take out the part of the code that isn't coupled to the framework. Make sure the code will be useful to all users, no matter what framework they put in front of it. The remaining part of the userland code that is coupled to the framework can be extracted into a framework-specific package, often known as a "bridge" package.

Looking at the framework-independent code that has now been extracted to a package, you can start applying the *Dependency Inversion* principle there and introduce interfaces and adapter code for concrete classes from libraries that your package uses. Figure 5-9 shows the dependency graph of the resulting packages when the userland code has been extracted and both a framework bridge and a library adapter have been added. The package can be used with framework X, but it should be easy to create another bridge package and make it work with framework Y too. The same goes for library A, for which an adapter is already available. It implements an interface from the package, making it easy to provide a second adapter that will make the package work with library B.

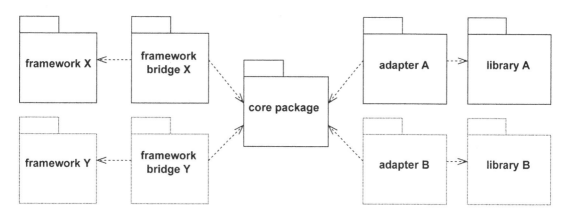

Figure 5-9. *The dependency graph after extracting a package and making it independent of the framework and libraries*

Not all third-party code requires you to apply the *Dependency Inversion* principle. If you'd never be allowed to depend on any third-party code directly, you'd have to reinvent everything again and again. In the next section, we enumerate the types of classes that definitely need an interface. What remains are classes that can be used as they are. In practice, I find that these will be classes that do one thing and do it well. Don't be afraid to depend on those, in particular if their maintainers do a good job in terms of package design.

Examples of third-party code you can depend on as they are can be found in libraries related to:

- Assertions

- Reflection

- Mapping

- Encoding/decoding

- Inflection

You'll likely be able to add some more examples. In practice, you may also decide to depend directly on other concrete third-party code, even though it would call for dependency inversion. You can always add an interface later, and for now enjoy building on top of other people's ready-to-use building blocks, sacrificing flexibility for an earlier release.

There's another option that you should think of when you consider using third-party code. Instead of working around their somewhat awkward API, or dealing with their unpredictable release cycle, you may also decide to copy their idea and build your own version of it. For example, if you need an event dispatcher, but none of the popular event dispatcher packages matches your expectations, consider writing one yourself. It isn't much code anyway, and by doing it, you can design it just the way you want it to be. It's not always the most efficient thing to do, but at least you have to consider it as a valid option. When reinventing the wheel, sometimes you end up with a better wheel.

When to Publish an Explicit Interface for a Class

In previous chapters, we've seen interfaces being used to make classes open for extension and closed for modification. We've learned how subclasses can be good substitutes for their interfaces. We've also discussed how to split interfaces according to how they are used. And finally we've learned how to invert dependency directions toward more abstract things. What we didn't discuss in detail is *which classes actually need an interface*. As mentioned several times before, not every class needs an interface. So before we wrap up this chapter and dive into the package design principles, let's first answer this question: when should you publish an explicit interface for a class? And when is a class without an interface sufficient?

If Not All Public Methods Are Meant to be Used by Regular Clients

A class always has an *implicit* interface, consisting of all its public methods. This is how the class will be known to other classes that use it. An implicit interface can easily be turned into an explicit one by collecting all those public methods (except for the constructor, which should not be considered a regular method), stripping the method bodies, and copying the remaining method signatures into an interface file (see Listing 5-21).

Listing 5-21. The Original EntityManager Class and its Extracted Explicit Interface

```
// the original class with only an implicit interface:

final class EntityManager
{
    public function persist(object $object): void
    {
```

```php
        // ...
    }

    public function flush(object $object = null): void
    {
        // ...
    }

    public function getConnection(): Connection
    {
        // ...
    }

    public function getCache(): Cache
    {
        // ...
    }

    // and so on
}

// the extracted - explicit - interface:

interface EntityManagerInterface
{
    public function persist(object $object): void;

    public function flush(object $object = null): void;

    public function getConnection(): Connection;

    public function getCache(): Cache;

    // ...
}
```

However, regular clients of `EntityManager` won't need access to the internally used `Connection` or `Cache` object, which can be retrieved by calling `getConnection()` or `getCache()`, respectively. You could even say that the *implicit* interface of the `EntityManager` class unnecessarily exposes implementation details and internal data structures to clients.

By copying the signatures of these methods to the newly created `EntityManagerInterface`, we missed the opportunity to limit the size of the interface as it gets exposed to regular clients. It would be most useful if clients only needed to depend on the methods they use. So the improved `EntityManagerInterface` should only keep `persist()` and `flush()`, as shown in Listing 5-22.

Listing 5-22. The Improved EntityManagerInterface

```
interface EntityManagerInterface
{
    public function persist(object $object);

    public function flush(object $object = null);
}
```

We've discussed this strategy in more detail in Chapter 4 when we covered the *Interface Segregation* principle, which tells you not to let clients depend on methods they don't use (or shouldn't use!).

If the Class Uses I/O

Whenever a class makes some call that uses I/O (the network, the filesystem, the system's source of randomness, or the system clock), you should definitely provide an interface for it. The reason being that in a test scenario, you want to replace that class with a test double and you need an interface for creating that test double. An example of a class that uses I/O is the `CurlHttpClient` in Listing 5-23.

Listing 5-23. The CurlHttpClient and its Interface

```
// a class that uses I/O:

final class CurlHttpClient
{
    public function get(string $url): string
```

```
    {
        $ch = curl_init();

        curl_setopt($ch, CURLOPT_URL, $url);
        curl_setopt($ch, CURLOPT_RETURNTRANSFER, true);

        // this call uses the network!
        $result = curl_exec($ch);

        // ...

        return $result;
    }
}

// an explicit interface for HTTP clients like CurlHttpClient

interface HttpClient
{
    public function get(string $url): string;
}
```

If you'd like to know more about using test doubles to replace actual I/O calls, take a look at my article series on "Mocking at Architectural Boundaries"[8].

If the Class Depends on Third-Party Code

If there is some third-party code (e.g., from a package you don't maintain yourself) that is used in your class, it can be wise to isolate the integration of your code with this third-party code and hide the details behind an interface. Good reasons to do so are:

- The (implicit) interface wouldn't be how you would've designed it yourself.

- You're not sure if the package is safe to rely on.

---

[8]"Mocking at architectural boundaries: persistence and time," https://matthiasnoback. nl/2018/02/mocking-at-architectural-boundaries-persistence-and-time/ "Mocking at architectural boundaries: the filesystem and randomness," https://matthiasnoback. nl/2018/03/mocking-the-filesystem-and-randomness/ and "Mocking the network," https://matthiasnoback.nl/2018/04/mocking-the-network/

Let's say you need a diffing tool to calculate the differences between two multi-line strings. There's an open source package (`nicky/funky-diff`) that provides more or less what you need, but the API is a bit off. You want a string with pluses and minuses, but the class in this package returns a list of `ChunkDiff` objects (see Listing 5-24).

Listing 5-24. The FunkyDiffer

```
class FunkyDiffer
{
    /**
     * @param array $from Lines
     * @param array $to Lines to compare to
     * @return array|ChunkDiff[]
     */
    public function diff(array $from, array $to)
    {
        // ...
    }
}
```

Besides offering a strange API, the package is being "maintained" by someone you've never heard of (and it has 15 open issues and 7 pull requests). So you need to protect the stability of your package and you define your own interface. Then you add an *Adapter* class[9] that implements *your* interface, yet delegates the work to the `FunkyDiffer` class, as shown in Listing 5-25.

Listing 5-25. An Adapter for the FunkyDiffer

```
interface Differ
{
    public function generate(string $from, string $to): string;
}
```

---

[9]Erich Gamma e.a., *Design Patterns: Elements of Reusable Object-Oriented Software*, Addison-Wesley, 1994.

```php
final class DifferUsesFunkyDiffer implements Differ
{
    private $funkyDiffer;

    public function __construct(FunkyDiffer $funkyDiffer)
    {
        $this->funkyDiffer = $funkyDiffer;
    }

    public function generate(string $from, string $to): string
    {
        return implode(
            "\n",
            array_map(
                function (ChunkDiff $chunkDiff) {
                    return $chunkDiff->asString();
                },
                $this->funkyDiffer->diff(
                    explode("\n", $from),
                    explode("\n", $to)
                )
            )
        );
    }
}
```

The advantage of this approach is that from now on you can always switch to a different library, without changing the bulk of your code. Only the adapter class needs to be rewritten to use that other library.

By the way, a good old *Façade*[10] might be an option here too (see Listing 5-26), since it would hide the use of the third-party implementation. However, due to the lack of an explicit interface, you wouldn't be able to experiment with alternative implementations. The same goes for the users of your package: they won't be able to write their own implementation of a "differ".

---

[10]Erich Gamma e.a., *Design Patterns: Elements of Reusable Object-Oriented Software*, Addison-Wesley, 1994.

Listing 5-26. A Façade for FunkyDiffer

```
final class Differ
{
    public function generate(string $from, string $to): string
    {
        $funkyDiffer = new FunkyDiffer();

        // delegate to FunkyDiffer
    }
}
```

If You Want to Introduce an Abstraction for Multiple Specific Things

If you want to treat different, specific classes in some way that is the same for every one of them, you should introduce an interface that covers their common ground. Such an interface is often called an "abstraction," because it abstracts away the details that don't matter to the client of that interface. A nice example is the VoterInterface from the Symfony Security component[11]. Every application has its own authorization logic, but Symfony's AccessDecisionManager[12] doesn't care about the exact rules. It can deal with any voter you write, as long as it implements VoterInterface and works according to the instructions provided by the documentation of that interface. An example of such an implementation is shown in Listing 5-27.

Listing 5-27. Example of a VoterInterface Implementation

```
final class MySpecificVoter implements VoterInterface
{
    public function vote(
        TokenInterface $token,
        $subject,
```

---

[11]https://symfony.com/doc/current/components/security/authorization.html

[12]https://github.com/symfony/security/blob/v4.1.6/Core/Authorization/
  AccessDecisionManager.php

```
        array $attributes
    ): int {
        // ...
    }
}
```

In the case of the `VoterInterface`, the package maintainers serve the users of their package by offering them a way to provide their own authorization rules. But sometimes an abstraction is only there for the code in the package itself. In that case too, don't hesitate to add it.

If You Foresee That the User Wants to Replace Part of the Object Hierarchy

In most cases, a `final class` is the best thing you can create. If a user doesn't like your class, they can simply choose not to use it. However, if you're building up a hierarchy of objects, you should introduce an interface for every class. That way the user can replace a particular piece of logic somewhere in that hierarchy with their own logic. It will make your code useful in as many situations as possible.

A nice example comes from Tactician[13], which offers a command bus implementation.

The package ships with a `CommandBus` class[14] (see Listing 5-28). It's a class, not an interface, because its implicit interface isn't larger than its explicit interface would be—the only public method is `handle()`.

Listing 5-28. The CommandBus Class (Abbreviated)

```
class CommandBus
{
    // ...

    public function __construct(array $middleware)
    {
        // ...
    }
```

---

[13]https://tactician.thephpleague.com/
[14]https://github.com/thephpleague/tactician/blob/v1.0.3/src/CommandBus.php

```
    public function handle($command)
    {
        // ...
    }

    // ...
}
```

To set up a working CommandBus instance, you need to instantiate a number of "middleware" classes that all implement the Middleware interface[15] (see Listing 5-29). This is an example of an interface that was introduced as an abstraction, allowing the package maintainer to treat multiple specific things in some generic way, as well as to allow users to plug in their own specific implementations.

Listing 5-29. The Middleware Interface (Abbreviated)

```
interface Middleware
{
    public function execute($command, callable $next);
}
```

One of these middleware interfaces is the CommandHandlerMiddleware[16], which itself needs a "command name extractor," a "handler locator," and a "method name inflector". All of which have a default implementation inside the package (the command name *is* the class name, the handler for a command is kept in memory, and the handle method is handle plus the name of the command), as shown in Listing 5-30.

Listing 5-30. Setting Up CommandHandlerMiddleware

```
$handlerMiddleware = new CommandHandlerMiddleware(
    new ClassNameExtractor(),
    new InMemoryLocator([...]),
    new HandleClassNameInflector()
);
```

---

[15]https://github.com/thephpleague/tactician/blob/v1.0.3/src/Middleware.php
[16]https://github.com/thephpleague/tactician/blob/v1.0.3/src/Handler/
CommandHandlerMiddleware.php

```
$commandBus = new CommandBus(
    [
        ...,
        $handlerMiddleware,
        ...
    ]
);
```

Each collaborating object that gets injected into CommandHandlerMiddleware can easily be replaced by re-implementing the interfaces of these objects (CommandNameExtractor, HandlerLocator, and MethodNameInflector, respectively). Because CommandHandlerMiddleware depends on interfaces, not on concrete classes, it will remain useful for its users, even if they want to replace part of the built-in logic with their own logic, such as when they would like to use their favorite service locator to retrieve the command handler from.

By the way, adding an interface for those collaborating objects also helps the user *decorate* existing implementations of the interface by using object composition.

For Everything Else: Stick to a Final Class

If your situation doesn't match any of the ones described previously, most likely the best thing you can do is *not* add an interface, and just stick to using a class, preferably a final class. The advantage of marking a class as "final" is that subclassing is no longer an officially supported way of modifying the behavior of a class. This saves you from a lot of trouble later on when you're changing that class as a package maintainer. You won't have to worry about users who rely on your class's internals in some unexpected way.

Classes that almost never need an interface are:

- Classes that model some concept from your domain (entities and value objects).

- Classes that otherwise represent stateful objects (as opposed to classes that represent stateless services).

- Classes that represent a particular piece of business logic, or a calculation.

What these types of classes have in common is that it's not at all needed nor desirable to swap their implementations out.

Conclusion

As we've seen in this chapter, following the *Dependency Inversion* principle is helpful when others start using your classes. They want your classes to be abstract, only depending on other abstract things, and leaving the details to a couple of small classes with specific responsibilities.

Applying the *Dependency Inversion* principle in your code will make it easy for users to swap out certain parts of your code with other parts that are tailored to their specific situation. At the same time, *your* code remains general and abstract and therefore highly reusable.

PART II

Package Design

Code consists of *statements*, grouped into *functions*, grouped into *classes*, grouped into *packages*, combined into *systems*. There are several insights about this chain of concepts that I would like to discuss here, before we dive into the actual *principles of package design*.

Becoming a Programmer

It occurred to me that in my programming career I learned about these different concepts in the exact same order in which I just mentioned them. The first thing I learned about PHP as a young website builder was to insert PHP statements into a regular HTML file. By doing so, it was possible to turn a static HTML page into a dynamic one. You could conditionally show some things on the page, dynamically build a navigation tree, do some form processing, and even fetch something from a database.

```php
<?php
$name = htmlentities($_GET['name'], ENT_QUOTES);
$day = date('l');
?>
<html>
    <head>
        <title>My first homepage</title>
    </head>
    <body>
        <h1>Welcome, <?=$name?></h1>
        <p>Today it's <?=$day?></p>
    </body>
</html>
```

When the pages I created became more complicated, I felt the need to organize things in a better way, to make my work easier and to support my future self when a client would change their mind again. At first I resorted to so-called include *files*. The behavior of those include files could be influenced using global variables:

```php
<?php
// display_day.php

global $day;

?><p>Today it's <?=$day?></p>
<?php
// index.php

global $day;

$day = date('l');
include('display_day.php');
```

Looking back at this strange code from my oldest projects, I realize that I was actually using those include files as some kind of *functions* (not in a truly functional manner though, because these "functions" had some nasty side effects, like sending output directly to the client).

Using include files as functions worked fine for some time, until customer requirements got more complicated and I had to build an authentication mechanism for users, using a login form. I copied some code from the Internet that contained some *actual functions*. Of course I just pasted the code in my project (and it worked). But then I started to unravel it, diving into this "new" concept of a function.

When I got it, things changed dramatically. On every opportunity to introduce a new function, I added one to a file called functions.php. This file was included in every PHP script, to make all those functions available everywhere:

```php
function wrap($text, $maxLineLength) {
    // ...
}

function fetch_user_data($id) {
    // ...
}
```

```
function array_merge_deep($array1, $array2) {
    // ...
}

function copy_shopping_cart() {
    // ...
}

function rename_file($source, $destination) {
    // ...
}

// ...
```

Even though many of those functions still echoed things directly to the client (instead of buffering the output), I felt that my applications were already becoming pretty advanced (of course, I copied this functions.php file into every new project I started).

At some point I was browsing through the php.net[1] website and stumbled upon the page about classes[2]. I recognized this "class" thing as a way of grouping functions that were related to each other. So I created a big Page class, which became the core of the first CMS I ever built. I've added the source of the Page class as an appendix to this book, for your enjoyment, but let me show you some of the more interesting parts of the code here.

```
class Page
{
  public $uri = null;
  public $page = array();
  public $site_title = ";
  public $breadcrumbs = array();
  public $js = array();
  public $css = array();
  public $auto_include_dir = ";
  /* @public $smart Smarty */
```

---

[1]https://secure.php.net/
[2]https://secure.php.net/manual/en/language.oop5.basic.php

```php
public $smarty = null;
public $default_template = ";
public $template = ";
public $cms_login = null;
public $user_login = null;
public $is_user = false;
public $is_admin = false;
public $languages = array();
public $default_language = null;
public $language = null;
public $menu_items = array();

protected $_extra_request_parameters = array();

public function __construct($uri)
{
  $this->connect_db();
  header('Content-Type: '.HEADER_CONTENT_TYPE);
  $this->smarty = new Smarty;

  if (isset($_GET['clear_cache']))
  {
    $this->smarty->clear_cache();
  }

  if (DEBUGGING)
  {
    $this->smarty->caching = false;
    if (trusted_ip())
    {
      $this->smarty->debugging = true;
    }
  }

  if (trusted_ip())
  {
    ini_set('display_errors', '1');
    error_reporting(
```

```php
            E_ERROR | E_PARSE | E_WARNING | E_USER_ERROR
            | E_USER_NOTICE | E_USER_WARNING
              );
    }
    else
    {
      $this->smarty->debugging = false;
      ini_set('display_errors', '0');
      error_reporting(0);
    }

    // ...

    if (!table_exists('content'))
    {
      require(ROOT.'/includes/install.php');
      install();
    }

    $this->add_title_part(SITE_TITLE);

    $this->cms_login = new LoginClass('admins', 'cms_login');
    $this->user_login = new LoginClass('users', 'user_login');

    if ($this->cms_login->isLoggedIn())
    {
      $this->is_admin = true;
    }

    if ($this->user_login->isLoggedIn())
    {
      $this->is_user = true;
    }

    // ...

    $this->open_page();
}
```

```
public function connect_db()
{
  $this->db_connection = @mysql_connect(
      MYSQL_HOST,
      MYSQL_USER,
      MYSQL_PASSWORD
      );

  if ($this->db_connection)
  {
    $this->db = @mysql_select_db(MYSQL_DB);
    if (!$this->db)
    {
      ?><p class="warning">Geen database!</p><?
      exit;
    }
  }
  else
  {
    ?><p class="warning">Geen verbinding!</p><?
    exit;
  }
}
}
```

Several highlights from this masterpiece:

- The Page class has about 20 or 30 instance variables.

- It depends on about 20 constants that are defined outside that class (more specifically, in the config.php file).

- It refers to so-called super-globals, like $_GET.

- It globally modifies the settings of the PHP process by configuring the PHP error mode in the constructor.

- Error messages (in Dutch) are being echoed directly to the user, after which the program simply terminates.

- It connects to a MySQL database and verifies that the required tables are there. If not, it runs the install script.

- It sends response headers.

Although I would never write such code today, when I look at the Page class now, I don't feel ashamed about what I did back then. It's clear to me that I wasn't struggling to get things *working* (because everything just worked; I always tried to do a good job in that respect). Rather, I was struggling to get things *organized*.

The Hardest Part

It took me a couple of years before I learned how to make my classes *moderately good*. And still every day there's something new to learn about class design, some old habit to drop, some new principle to apply. From this I draw the conclusion that organizing code into classes is a *difficult thing*. It's fairly easy to learn all there is to know about the keywords that a programming language provides for working with classes (class, extends, implements, abstract, final, etc.). Learning how to use them well—that's much harder.

Let's get back to this chain of concepts: statements, grouped into functions, grouped into classes, grouped into packages, combined in a system. Let me ask: what is the "meat" of a program? Well, it's the *statements*. Statements actually make things happen. If we were to transform all class methods of a program to regular functions and then inline those functions, we'd get one long page of statements and, when executed, the program would still do the same thing.

From this we can draw the conclusion that code does not *need* to be organized if you only need to make it *just work*. For the computer, what counts is statements. Still, we make great efforts to *modularize* our statements. We put them in class methods, and we group the classes together in packages. And judging by the order in which you learn things as a developer, writing classes and creating packages is much more difficult than writing just statements.

Principles of Cohesion

Over the years you struggle to organize your code in the best way possible. While doing so, you'll gradually develop a strong sense of "belonging together". It'll help you decide whether or not two pieces of code belong together. This intuition keeps evolving forever: when you're writing statements and put them into functions, when you write classes for those functions, and when you combine those classes into packages.

This intuition you have as a programmer, this sense of "belonging together," is actually about something called *cohesion*. Cohesion is a *degree of relatedness*. Some things are highly cohesive, and some are less cohesive, depending on how much they are related to each other.

Early in life you learn to determine whether or not things are cohesive. In school you get these little exercises: "One of the following words does not belong in the list, which is it? Duck, frog, fish, camel." When you have the list "duck, frog, fish," you have a highly cohesive list of words. The words stand for things that are highly related to each other (because they are all names of animals that live or survive in water). When you add "camel" to the list, it definitely becomes less cohesive. This resembles your job as a programmer: you need to find out which things you can add without making the whole *less cohesive*, and which things you can remove to make the whole *more cohesive*.

In the context of package design, cohesion is mainly about which classes belong together in a package. There are many different ways in which you can arrange and combine classes and all of them produce a different kind of cohesion. For example, you can group all classes that serve as a controller, or all classes that are entities. The result is something called *logical cohesion*. But when you group the "blog post" controller and the "blog post" entity, the result is *communicational cohesion:* all classes in such a package operate on the same data, i.e. blog post records from the database.

There are several other types of cohesion (sequential, temporal, etc.), but the most important type of cohesion, the one you should strive for, is *functional cohesion*. Functional cohesion is achieved when all things in a "module" (e.g., a package) together can be used to perform a single, well-defined task.

Class Design Principles Benefit Cohesion

Earlier I said that the programmer's sense of belonging together was based on intuition, shaped by experience. Of course there's also a rational side of that sense: if you know about class design principles then that will help you write highly cohesive code. For example, when you apply the SOLID principles to your classes, they will automatically become more cohesive:

- You will end up with classes having fine-grained, client-specific interfaces, which makes it unlikely that those interfaces contain methods that don't belong there. So applying the *Interface Segregation* principle will give you highly cohesive classes.

- You will also have classes with just one reason for change, which means they are not "all over the place". So applying the *Single Responsibility* principle also has the beneficial effect of making classes more cohesive.

Once we know how to create highly cohesive classes, we can take the next step. After statements, functions, and classes we arrive at packages. Packages are groups of classes, and just like everything that is a group of things, a package has cohesion (a certain degree of relatedness) too. If classes were grouped arbitrarily, the package containing them would have *coincidental cohesion*. Of course, the trick is to group classes in such a way that the package has a high level of functional cohesion: all the classes in the package should serve to perform a single, well-defined task.

There are three package design principles that support you in creating highly cohesive packages. In the following chapters, we will discuss each of them extensively. They are called, respectively, the *Release/Reuse Equivalence* principle (Chapter 6), the *Common Reuse* principle (Chapter 7) and the *Common Closure* principle (Chapter 8). Applying these principles will lead to smaller packages that are easier to maintain and use.

Focusing on the package and its degree of cohesion is important, but it's equally important to consider how the package behaves in relation to other packages—in other words, how it's coupled to them.

Principles of Coupling

Most classes can't survive on their own: they have some kind of a dependency and most likely even multiple dependencies. Maybe they need an instance of another class to delegate some of the work. Or they *produce* instances of another class. In other words, many classes depend on other classes, which actually couples them to each other.

As we saw in the first part of this book, applying the SOLID principles to class design has a healthy effect on coupling between classes. As you may remember, according to the *Dependency Inversion* principle, a class should only depend on another class or interface that is abstract, not concrete. It should also not depend on lower-level classes, only on high-level classes. And according to the *Open/Closed* principle, a class should be open for extension, but closed for modification, which means that its behavior should be modifiable, without actually modifying its code.

When we discussed the Dependency Inversion principle, we already briefly considered the situation in which one class depends on a class in another package. A class from one package that depends on a class from another package introduces a new level of coupling, called *package coupling*.

If you've worked with packages and a dependency or package manager, you already know that package coupling can go wrong in many ways. Often you get into trouble because of incompatible dependency versions. Or somehow circular dependencies occur. Maybe unstable packages that are liable to change cause your own project to break frequently. Or maybe some of your dependencies have unstable dependencies themselves, the effects of which ripple through to your own code.

Because of these problems, we are in need of some guiding principles that help us design packages that have good dependencies. We need packages that can be trustworthy dependencies of other packages and projects. The relevant package design principles are called "principles of coupling" and we discuss them in the last three chapters: the *Acyclic Dependencies* principle (Chapter 9), the *Stable Dependencies* principle (Chapter 10), and the *Stable Abstractions* principle (Chapter 11), after we've covered the cohesion principles in full.

## CHAPTER 6

The Release/Reuse Equivalence Principle

The first of the actual package design principles discussed in this book is the *Release/ Reuse Equivalence* principle. This principle says[1]:

> *The granule of reuse is the granule of release.*

This principle has two sides. First of all, you should only release as much code as you (or others) can reasonably reuse. It makes no sense to invest all the time and energy needed to properly release code if nobody is going to use it in another project anyway. This may require you to do some kind of research to establish the viability of your package once you would privately or publicly release it. Maybe the package only *seems to be reusable*, but in the end it turns out to be useful in your specific use case only.

The other side of the principle is that you can only reuse the amount of code that you can *actually release*. By applying all the principles of class design, you may have created perfectly generic, reusable code. But if you never release that code, then it's not reusable after all. So before you start making all your code reusable, try to answer this question first: are you going to be able to release that code and manage future releases too?

Being aware of the effort that's required to release a package will help you decide on the number and the size of the packages that you're going to create. Releasing hundreds of tiny packages is something you can't possibly do. Each package requires a certain amount of time and energy from its maintainer. Think about tracking and fixing issues, adding version tags to new releases, keeping the documentation up-to-date, etc. On the other hand, releasing one very big package is equally impossible. It will undergo so many

---

[1]Robert C. Martin, "The principles of OOD," `http://butunclebob.com/ArticleS.UncleBob.PrinciplesOfOod`

© Matthias Noback 2018
M. Noback, *Principles of Package Design*, https://doi.org/10.1007/978-1-4842-4119-6_6

changes related to different parts of the package that it will be a very volatile package, a constantly moving target. This is not helpful at all for its users.

As I explained in the Introduction, cohesion is always about "belonging together". And so the cohesion principles of package design offer strategies to decide if classes should be grouped in a package. The *Release/Reuse Equivalence* principle helps you decide *if* you would be able to release such a package at all. It makes you aware of the fact that a released package requires the careful nurturing of its maintainer.

The remaining sections of this chapter will give you an overview of all the things you need to take care of when you start releasing packages. While the previous part of the book was about the way in which you can prepare your *classes* for reuse, this chapter is about how you can prepare your *package* of classes to be reused, that is, to be released.

Although we'll talk about code and discuss tactics for keeping it backward compatible, you should know that the other half of this chapter covers other, more practical, topics related to package design, like semantic versioning, quality assurance, and metafiles that need to be present in a package. If you're not (yet) interested in these topics, either because you know about them already, or you want to dig into them only when you're actually starting to release a package, feel free to skip the following sections and go straight to the Conclusion of this chapter.

Keep Your Package Under Version Control

The first thing you need to do is set up a version control system for your package. You need to be able to keep track of changes by you or any of the contributors, and people need to be able to pull in the latest version of the package. So even though mailing around code snippets would technically be a kind of version control (the sent date of the message could be used as the version number of the package), you should always use a *real* version control system (like Git[2]).

If you have an idea for a package (which would primarily be a coherent set of classes), the first thing you do is set up a version control repository for it. This will enable you to revert to previous situations if one particular change endangered the whole project. If you work in a team, using version control also helps you prevent conflicting changes. It enables you to work on and test a new or experimental feature in a separate *branch*, without jeopardizing the stability of the master branch of the package.

---

[2]https://git-scm.com/

The version control repository should be treated as a full description of the *history* of the project. You and your team are going to use the version control repository as a way to figure out when or why a bug was introduced. Make sure to only commit changes to the repository that are cohesive (i.e., belong together) and add explanatory comments when you commit something.

In order to make your package available, you have to make sure it's hosted somewhere. Depending on your needs, this can be something public or private, hosted or self-hosted.

Add a Package Definition File

Most programming languages have a standardized way of defining packages. And often this is just a simple file that provides some or all of the following properties of the package:

- Name of the package

- Maintainers, possibly some contributors

- URL and type of the version control repository

- Required dependencies, like other packages, specific language versions, etc.

Read as much as you can about your different options. A package containing a rich definition file that utilizes all the options in the right way is likely to be a well-behaving package in the package ecosystem of your programming language.

Once you've created a correct package definition file, you probably have to register the package to some sort of a central package repository or registry. Each programming language has its own remote package repositories, with different manuals and requirements.

Use Semantic Versioning

When you release a package, you have to answer the following questions and make your intentions clear:

- Do you introduce changes in the API of your code with great care?

- Will you try to make sure that those changes don't break the way in which users interact with your package?

- In which situations would you allow yourself to heavily change your API?

In other words, how're you going to take care of *backward compatibility*? Package maintainers generally follow a versioning strategy called "semantic versioning". The outline of this strategy is the following:

- Fix bugs and release them as *patch* versions (e.g., x.x.1 ⇒ x.x.2).

- Add new things to your package, but make sure to release a new *minor* version each time you do so (e.g., x.1.x ⇒ x.2.x). When you want to deprecate things, just keep them around for a while.

- Remove deprecated parts or introduce backward incompatible changes when you release a new *major* version (e.g., 1.x.x ⇒ 2.x.x).

The first part of a package's version number, the number before the first dot, is called the *major version*. The first major version is usually 0. This version should be considered unfinished, experimental, heavily changing without too much care for backward compatibility. Starting from major version 1, the public API is supposed to be stabilized and the package has a certain trustworthiness from that moment on. Each subsequent increment of the major version number marks the moment that part of the code breaks backward compatibility. It's the moment when method signatures change, and deprecated classes or interfaces are removed. Sometimes even a complete rework of the same functionality is being released as a new *major* version.

The second part of the version number is the *minor version*. It also starts counting from 0, though this has no special significance, except "being the first". Minor versions can be incremented when new functionality has been added to the package or when parts of the existing public API have been marked as deprecated. The promise of a new minor version is that nothing will change for its users, existing ways in which they use the package will not be broken. A minor version only *adds* new ways of using the package.

The last part of the version number is the *patch version*. Starting with version 0, it gets incremented for each patch that is released for the package. This can be either a bug fix, or some refactored private code, i.e. code that's not accessible by just using the public API of the package. Since refactoring means changing the structure of code without changing its behavior, refactoring private package code will not have any negative side-effect on existing users.

Immediately after the version number (consisting of the major, minor and patch version, separated by dots), there may be a textual indication of the state of the package: alpha, beta, rc (release candidate), optionally followed by another dot and another incremental number.

The number combined with the optional meta-identifier can be used to compare version numbers. Listing 6-1 shows a sorted list of version numbers.

Listing 6-1. Sorted Version Numbers

```
1.9.10
2.0.0
2.1.0
2.1.1-alpha
2.1.1-beta
2.1.1-rc.1
2.1.1-rc.2
2.1.1
```

Comparison is done in the natural way, so 2.1.1 is a lower version than 2.10.1. There's no limit to each part of the version number, so you can just keep incrementing it.

Design for Backward Compatibility

When you use semantic versioning for your packages, providing backward compatibility means that you strive to provide the exact same functionality in minor version x + 1 as in the previous minor version x. In other words, if some user's code relies on a feature provided by version 1.1.0, you promise that this same feature will be available in 1.2.0. Using it will have exactly the same effects in both versions. Not only would it have the same behavioral effects, the feature can also still be invoked in the same way.

Of course, you may have fixed some bugs between two minor versions, and you may have *added* some features. But none of these things should pose any problems for users who upgrade their dependency on your package to the next minor version. All their tests should still pass, and everything should still work as it did before upgrading the dependency.

As you can imagine, providing *true* backward compatibility can be really hard. You want to make some progress, but your promise for backward compatibility can hold you back. Still, if you want your package to be used by other developers, you need to give them both new features *and* continuity.

There's a time when you don't *have* to provide the continuity, which is when your package's major version is still 0.x.x. During this period, your package will be considered unstable anyway and you can move everything around. This may enrage some early adopters, but since they are aware of the fact that the package is still unstable, they can't complain really.

Working forever on 0.* versions of a package would seem to alleviate you from the pain of keeping backward compatibility. However, an *unstable* package will likely not be used in any serious project that itself intends to be *stable*. In such a project, people would get really mad when they upgrade such a package and nothing works anymore. They would have to add extra integration tests, to test the boundaries between their and your code, so they will notice any compatibility problems early on. They will be scared to upgrade your package and therefore also miss all relevant bug or security vulnerability fixes.

In conclusion, you should make up your mind about the design of your code and, as soon as you have tested your package in one or two of your projects, release it as version 1.0.0. If you then really hate the design of your code, your strategy could be to start working on version 2.0.0 and announce that you will stop developing features for version 1.0 soon. Using version control branches, you would still be able to provide fixes for the previous major version if you want.

Rules of Thumb

Even though you could get away with only releasing major versions, the more likely scenario is that you will release minor versions too. So designing for backward compatibility should be part of your strategy from the moment you release the first major version of your package. In the following sections, I discuss some things you should and should not do in order to provide backward compatibility.

These are just examples and rules of thumb. There are many more ways in which you can prevent a backward compatibility break and still they can accidentally happen. Software is already complex by nature, but there are also ways in which people use your code that you don't officially support, or don't know of yet. This means you will never be fully covered. But you can at least minimize the potential damage.

Don't Throw Anything Away

Whenever you add something to your package, make sure it still exists in the next version. This applies to things like:

- Classes

- Methods

- Functions

- Parameters

- Constants

A class *exists* if it can be auto-loaded, so classes don't necessarily need to be in the same file. Just make sure the class loader is always able to find them. This means you may move a class to another package and add that package as a dependency.

When You Rename Something, Add a Proxy

Renaming classes is possible, but make sure that the old class can still be instantiated (see Listing 6-2).

Listing 6-2. The Old Class Is Still Available

```
/**
 * @deprecated Use NewClass instead
 */
class DeprecatedClass extends NewClass
{
    // will inherit all methods from NewClass
}
```

```
class NewClass
{
    // ...
}
```

This may require you to temporarily remove the `final` keyword from the declaration of the old class, or instead use object composition as an alternative approach to keeping compatibility.

Renaming a method is possible, but make sure you forward the call to the new method (see Listing 6-3).

Listing 6-3. The Old Method Is Still Available

```
class SomeClass
{
    /**
     * @deprecated use newMethod() instead
     */
    public function deprecatedMethod()
    {
        return $this->newMethod();
    }

    public function newMethod()
    {
        // ...
    }
}
```

Or if you have moved the functionality to another class, make sure it still works when someone uses the old method (see Listing 6-4).

Listing 6-4. The Old Method Is A Proxy for the New Method

```php
class SomeClass
{
    /**
     * @deprecated Use Something::doComplicated() instead
     */
    public function doSomethingComplicated()
    {
        $something = new Something();

        return $something->doComplicated();
    }
}
```

ADD @DEPRECATED ANNOTATIONS

Whenever you deprecate an element of your code, be it a class, a method, a function, or a
property, you should not remove it immediately, but keep it around until you release the next
major version. In the meantime, make sure it has the @deprecated annotation. Don't forget
to add a little explanation and tell the users what they should do instead, or how they can
modify their own code to make it ready for the next major version in which the deprecated
things will be removed.

Renaming parameters of a method is not problematic (in PHP at least), as long as
their order and type doesn't change. Renaming parameters of a method defined in an
interface is also not problematic. Classes that implement an interface may always use
different names, as long as the parameter types correspond (see Listing 6-5).

Listing 6-5. Renaming Parameters Is Fine, as Long as Their Types Are the Same

```php
// interface defined inside the package
interface SomeInterface
{
    public function doSomething(ObjectManager $objectManager);
}
```

```
// class created by a user of the package
class SomeClass implements SomeInterface
{
    public function doSomething(ObjectManager $entityManager)
    {
        // ...
    }
}
```

Only Add Parameters to the End and with a Default Value

When you need to add a parameter to a method, make sure you add it to the end of the existing list of parameters. Also make sure that the new parameter has a sensible default value (see Listing 6-6).

Listing 6-6. Only Add New Parameters with a Default Value to the End of the Method Signature

```
// current version
class StorageHandler
{
    public function persist(object $object): void
    {
        $this->entityManager->persist($object);

        /*
         * The current implementation always flushes
         * the entity manager
         */
        $this->entityManager->flush();
    }
}

// next version
class StorageHandler
{
    public function persist(
```

```
        object $object,
        $andFlush = true
    ): void {
        $this->entityManager->persist($object);

        // the new implementation only flushes if requested
        if ($andFlush) {
            $this->entityManager->flush();
        }
    }
}
```

The extra parameter $andFlush has been introduced with a default value of true to make sure that the new method behaves exactly the same as the old method, which already flushed the entity manager by default.

Methods Should Not Have Implicit Side-Effects

Don't expect the users of your code to rely on a particular implicit side-effect of calling a method. When you later change the code, the side-effect may disappear, which breaks the user's code. See Listing 6-7 for an example of this.

Listing 6-7. Example Side-Effect That Disappears in a Later Version of the Method

```
// previous version
class Stream
{
    public function open(string $file): void
    {
        /*
         * The previous implementation creates a directory
         * if necessary
         */
        $this->createDirectoryIfNotExists($file);

        $this->handle = fopen($file, 'w');
    }
```

```php
    private function createDirectoryIfNotExists(
        string $file
    ): void {
        // ...
    }
}

// next version
class Stream
{
    public function open(string $file): void
    {
        /*
         * The new implementation does not create a directory
         * automatically
         */
        $this->handle = fopen($file, 'w');
    }
}
```

In the previous version, Stream::open() implicitly created a directory when a file
was opened. This behavior turned out to be problematic in some situations, so the next
version of Stream::open() leaves it to the user to make sure the directory exists. Users
can use Filesystem::isDirectory() and Filesystem::createDirectory()
(see Listing 6-8).

Listing 6-8. The Filesystem Class

```php
class Filesystem
{
    public function createDirectory(string $directory): void
    {
        // ...
    }
```

```
public function isDirectory(string $directory): bool
{
    // ...
}
}
```

Of course this change causes a backward compatibility break. But this could have been prevented in the first place; make sure every method has no hidden side-effects and does one thing, and one thing only. Define that one thing clearly in the method's documentation.

Dependency Versions Should Be Permissive

If your package has some dependencies itself, make sure you don't put too many restrictions on their version numbers. For instance, when you write the code for a new package you may prefer to work with the latest version of one of its dependencies; let's say that's version 2.4.3.

If the maintainer of that package has taken proper care of backward compatibility, it's likely that your package works well with version 2.3, and maybe even with 2.2 or 2.1. However, by requiring version 2.4.3 or higher of the dependency, you have effectively excluded all users who have lower versions of that same dependency installed in their project, even though your package would work fine with these older versions.

There are two solutions—force your users to upgrade to a new version of that dependency or make your own requirements less restrictive. Since the first option may break things in their project (a pain of which you don't want to be the cause), it's almost always best to choose the second option—make your code compatible with older versions and loosen your own requirements.

This is also true the other way around: if a new stable version of a package becomes available. As a package maintainer you are expected to make your package work with that new version too. You should check if it already does by installing the new version of the dependency and running the tests of your package. If necessary, make some changes to your code until all the tests pass. Of course, you need to make sure that the package continues to work with the previous version of the dependency. You might set up some continuous integration process (we'll get back to that) to do this automatically for you.

Use Objects Instead of Primitive Values

In order to provide backward compatibility, it's a good idea to use objects where you would normally use arrays or primitive-type values. Consider the incremental changes to HttpClientInterface shown in Listing 6-9.

Listing 6-9. Incremental Changes to HttpClientInterface

```
// version 1.0.0
interface HttpClientInterface
{
    public function connect(string $host): void;
}

// version 1.1.0
interface HttpClientInterface
{
    public function connect(
        string $hostname,
        int $port = 80
    ): void;
}

// version 1.2.0
interface HttpClientInterface
{
    public function connect(
        string $hostname,
        int $port = 80,
        bool $useTls = false
    ): void;
}

// version 1.3.0
interface HttpClientInterface
{
    public function connect(
        string $hostname,
```

```
        int $port = 80,
        bool $useTls = false,
        bool $verifyPeer = true
    ): void;
}
```

Instead of adding more and more parameters with default values, it would be much easier if connect() would have a single parameter from the start, which could itself be expanded without breaking backward compatibility. We could combine all these separate values (hostname, port, etc.) into one easy-to-upgrade object called ConnectionConfiguration (see Listing 6-10).

Listing 6-10. HttpClientInterface Accepts a Single Configuration Object

```
interface HttpClientInterface
{
    public function connect(
        ConnectionConfiguration $configuration
    ): void;
}
```

By doing so, subsequent upgrades of the package won't need to change the signature of the connect() method, but will only add new settings to the ConnectionConfiguration class (see Listing 6-11).

Listing 6-11. Incremental Changes to ConnectionConfiguration

```
// version 1.0.0
class ConnectionConfiguration
{
    private $hostname;

    public function __construct(string $hostname)
    {
        $this->hostname = $hostname;
    }
```

```php
    public function getHostname(): string
    {
        return $this->hostname;
    }
}

// version 1.1.0
class ConnectionConfiguration
{
    // ...

    private $port = 80;

    public function getPort(): int
    {
        return $this->port;
    }

    public function setPort(int $port): void
    {
        $this->port = $port;
    }
}

// version 1.2.0
class ConnectionConfiguration
{
    // ...

    private $useTls = false;

    public function shouldUseTls(): bool
    {
        return $this->useTls;
    }
```

```php
    public function useTls(bool $useTls): void
    {
        $this->useTls = $useTls;
    }
}

// version 1.3.0
class ConnectionConfiguration
{
    // ...

    private $verifyPeer = false;

    public function shouldVerifyPeer(): bool
    {
        return $this->verifyPeer;
    }

    public function verifyPeer(bool $verifyPeer): void
    {
        $this->verifyPeer = $verifyPeer;
    }
}
```

Users of this package would not get in trouble when the maintainer adds an extra setting to ConnectionConfiguration, as long as it has a sensible default value.

Use Objects for Encapsulation of State and Behavior

Using an object instead of a primitive-type value like we did in the example of the ConnectionConfiguration is not only useful when you're aiming for making backward compatible changes to a method signature. An object's natural encapsulation of implementation details also helps you maintain backward compatibility.

Take for example the constructor of ConnectionConfiguration. At one point in time it wasn't possible to separately configure the port—it was extracted from the hostname instead. In a later version of the class, the setPort() method was added, but to maintain backward compatibility, the old logic for extracting the port from the hostname is still there (see Listing 6-12).

Listing 6-12. setHostname() Supports Some Old Behavior

```
class ConnectionConfiguration
{
    private $hostname;
    private $port = 80;

    public function setHostname(string $hostname): void
    {
        // for backward compatibility, extract the port
        // from the hostname, if applicable:
        if (strpos($hostname, ':') !== false) {
            list($hostname, $port) = explode($hostname);
            $this->setPort($port);
        }

        $this->hostname = $host;
    }

    public function setPort(int $port): void
    {
        if ($port <= 0) {
            throw new InvalidArgumentException(
                Port should be larger than 0
            );
        }

        $this->port = $port;
    }

    // ...
}
```

Supporting different types of arguments can also be a great way to normalize data and keep backward compatibility over time. For example, you can upgrade a parameter type from a single value to a list of values by leaving out the type (or overloading the method if your language supports it), without breaking backward compatibility. Or you could upgrade a primitive-type value to an object if the client still uses a primitive-type value but internally you already use a proper object. Both examples are shown in Listing 6-13.

Listing 6-13. Supporting Different Argument Types

```php
/**
 * @param string|array $emailAddresses
 */
public function setTo($emailAddresses): void
{
    if (!is_array($emailAddresses)) {
        $emailAddresses = [$emailAddresses];
    }

    // ...
}

/**
 * @param int|DateTimeImmutable $time
 */
public function setLastModified($time): void
{
    if (is_int($time)) {
        $time = DateTimeImmutable::createFromFormat('U', $time);
    }

    if (!$time instanceof DateTimeImmutable) {
        throw new \InvalidArgumentException(...);
    }

    // ...
}
```

Use Object Factories

It's likely that between different package versions, a class will have different dependencies. Consider the Validator class in Listing 6-14. The initial version of this class requires no constructor arguments at all. A later version has been "internationalized" and consequently requires a Translator service to be injected.

Listing 6-14. In the Next Version, the Validator Class Has an Extra Constructor Argument

```
// version 1.0.0, no constructor arguments
class Validator
{
    public function __construct()
    {
        // ...
    }
}

// usage:
$validator = new Validator();

// version 2.0.0, added one constructor argument
class Validator
{
    public function __construct(Translator $translator)
    {
        // ...
    }
}

// usage:
$validator = new Validator(new Translator());
```

When users upgrade the validator package from version 1.0.0 to 2.0.0, their application will be broken because they don't provide that extra constructor argument yet.

To prevent such backward compatibility breaks, it would be better if we had provided a factory for `Validator` objects from the start. This way, users only need to create a factory (which should require no constructor arguments), and from then on they could use the factory to create a new validator (see Listing 6-15).

Listing 6-15. The ValidatorFactory Class

```
class ValidatorFactory
{
    public function createValidator(): Validator
    {
        $translator = new Translator();

        return new Validator($translator);
    }
}

// usage:
$validator = (new ValidatorFactory())->createValidator();
```

If in a future version, the `Validator` class would need any other constructor argument, the factory will add it behind the scenes and the user wouldn't need to know about it. Again, the trick is called "encapsulation": this time `ValidatorFactory` *encapsulates the creation logic* of `Validator`.

And So On...

By now you probably get the idea. There are many ways in which you can make your code backward compatible and still allow for future changes. For more on this subject I would like to point you to an article by Garrett Rooney entitled "Preserving Backward Compatibility".[3] He describes many interesting ways in which developers of the Subversion project have tried to maintain backward compatibility, while enabling *forward compatibility*. Another interesting document is "Our Backward Compatibility Promise"[4] delivered by the Symfony framework team. It may become a good guide for you too. One last suggestion: for PHP, there's a tool called Roave Backward Compatibility Check[5] that can analyze the code in a repository and find out if it introduces any backward compatibility breaks. It provides a detailed overview of the changes to the API

---

[3]Garrett Rooney, "Preserving Backward Compatibility," `https://web.archive.`
`org/web/20180121015221/http://www.onlamp.com/pub/a/onlamp/2005/02/17/`
`backwardscompatibility.html` (the original page is no longer available)

[4]`https://symfony.com/doc/current/contributing/code/bc.html`

[5]`https://github.com/Roave/BackwardCompatibilityCheck`

of your package and how these changes may break client code. This could spare you from a lot of time and frustration later on.

Finally, there's a meta-perspective that you have to take into consideration while doing all this work to prevent backward compatibility breaks. If *backward compatibility* is your main concern when working on your packages, it will be very hard to move forward. As Anthony Ferrara puts it:

> *[...] every release adds more cruft for you to maintain. Over time this creates a halting effect on the code base involved that makes it nearly impossible to clean up and "make things better. [...] So next time you want to propose a change, rather than thinking how it can break BC, try thinking how you can make the change compatible with future use cases and changes. The best way to prevent BC breaks is to plan for them from the beginning.*[6]

Add Metafiles

The metafiles that are absolutely necessary are a quick start guide in the form of a README file and some legal stuff in the form of a license file.

README and Documentation

The README file should be in the root directory of the package. It contains everything a user needs to get started. The README file may be the only official documentation for a package. If not, it should contain a link to some other source of documentation inside the package (for instance, in its docs directory) or a dedicated website. Whichever strategy you choose, the README file is *mandatory* since it's the starting point for people to learn more about your package.

A README file is a text file. The lines should be wrapped at an appropriate width (e.g., 80 columns) in order to make it readable in the terminal. It's also a good idea to apply some styling and structuring to it. It's fairly conventional to write the file in Markdown,[7] which gives you some basic markup options. You can write some words in italics or bold, add code blocks, and use section headers. If you use Markdown in your README file, rename the file to README.md.

The README file should at least contain the following sections.

---

[6]Anthony Ferrara, "Backwards Compatibility Is For Suckers," https://blog.ircmaxell.com/2013/06/backwards-compatibility-is-for-suckers.html

[7]https://daringfireball.net/projects/markdown/syntax

Installation and Configuration

This can be as simple as mentioning the command by which you can install the package in a PHP project, for example:

```
composer require matthiasnoback/some-package
```

Then tell the users everything else they need to do in order to use the package. Maybe they need to set up or configure some things, clear a cache, add some tables to a database, etc.

Usage

You need to show users how they can use the code in your package. This requires a quick explanation of some use cases and *code samples* for those situations. Packages often contain a separate directory with (working) sample code too.

Extension Points (Optional)

If the package is designed to be extended, if there are plugins for it, or bundles/modules that make it easy to integrate the library in a framework-based project, make sure you mention those *extension points*.

Limitations (Optional)

You should mention use cases for which the package currently offers no solution. You should also mention known problems (bugs or other limitations) and maybe some features that you intend to implement some time.

License

Another file that is mandatory is the LICENSE file. Even though you have possibly already provided the *name* of the license that applies to your package in the package definition file, you should still add the *full* license to your package. It should be in a file called

LICENSE in the root of the package. A very common license for open source software is the MIT license[8] (see Listing 6-16).

Listing 6-16. The MIT License

```
Copyright (c) <year(s)> <name(s)>

Permission is hereby granted, free of charge, to any person
obtaining a copy of this software and associated documentation
files (the "Software"), to deal in the Software without
restriction, including without limitation the rights to use,
copy, modify, merge, publish, distribute, sublicense, and/or
sell copies of the Software, and to permit persons to whom
the Software is furnished to do so, subject to the following
conditions:

The above copyright notice and this permission notice shall
be included in all copies or substantial portions of the
Software.

THE SOFTWARE IS PROVIDED "AS IS", WITHOUT WARRANTY OF ANY
KIND, EXPRESS OR IMPLIED, INCLUDING BUT NOT LIMITED TO THE
WARRANTIES OF MERCHANTABILITY, FITNESS FOR A PARTICULAR
PURPOSE AND NONINFRINGEMENT. IN NO EVENT SHALL THE AUTHORS
OR COPYRIGHT HOLDERS BE LIABLE FOR ANY CLAIM, DAMAGES OR
OTHER LIABILITY, WHETHER IN AN ACTION OF CONTRACT, TORT OR
OTHERWISE, ARISING FROM, OUT OF OR IN CONNECTION WITH THE
SOFTWARE OR THE USE OR OTHER DEALINGS IN THE SOFTWARE.
```

If you wonder why it's important to have a license file in your package, it depends on the country you live in, but some companies need your explicit permission to use your code in the way they intend to. They want to prevent legally uncomfortable situations caused by accidental copyright infringement. Equally important is that it relieves you of any damage your code may cause when used by somebody else.

---

[8]https://opensource.org/licenses/MIT

Change Log (Optional)

Besides the mandatory README and LICENSE files, you should also consider adding a change log. This will make it easy for users to find out what has changed between versions of the package. Based on the information, they can decide if it's necessary or useful for them to upgrade their installed version of the package.

Each new version (major, minor or patch) gets its own section in the change log in which you describe the changes that were made since the previous version. You should briefly describe new features that were added, things that were deprecated (but not removed), and problems that were fixed, as well as possibly point to issues in the issue tracker. See Listing 6-17 for an example of a CHANGELOG.md file.

Listing 6-17. An Excerpt from a CHANGELOG.md File

```
# Changelog

## v0.5.0

- Automatically resolve a definition's class before comparing
it to the expected class.

## v0.4.0

- Added `ContainerBuilderHasSyntheticServiceConstraint` and
corresponding assertion (as suggested by @WouterJ).

...
```

There is no standard format, although the one proposed on keepachangelog.com[9] is both simple and complete.

Upgrade Notes (Optional)

Each section of the change log may contain some upgrade notes that tell users what they need to do when they upgrade to a newer version. For instance, if some classes were deprecated, it's a good idea to mention in the change log in which version you actually removed them.

---

[9]https://keepachangelog.com/

In some cases, these upgrade notes start taking up too much space, which will muddle the view on the actual change log. Then it's time to move the upgrade notes to specific UPGRADE-x files. For example, UPGRADE-3.md will contain instructions for upgrading the dependency on this package from version 2.x.x to 3.x.x. Remember that in between major versions no actions from the user should be required, because minor and patch versions only introduce backward compatible changes.

Guidelines for Contributing (Optional)

In particular, if your project is an open source project, you may consider adding a separate file in which you describe the process of contributing to the package. This file should contain things like:

- Suggestions on how to install the package in such a way that you can run its test suite and start working on a new feature, bug fix, etc.

- Guidelines for submitting your work to the project (requirements for the pull request description, coding style, etc.).

- How to reach out for help, where to discuss issues, etc.

Quality Control

We already discussed many characteristics of a package that would make it qualify as a good package (or a "good product"). Most of these characteristics were related to the infrastructure of the package: a package should display some good manners when it comes to version control, the package definition file, dependencies and their versions, and backward compatibility. Several metafiles need to be in place, for the package to be usable, like documentation and a license file, etc.

You may have noticed that until now we haven't given much attention to the actual code in your package. We will of course discuss the required characteristics of classes in a package at great length in the next chapters. But in the last sections of this chapter, I first point out some aspects of the package infrastructure that will help you create packages with high-quality code.

Quality from the User's Point of View

A package makes some implicit promises about the code it contains. It basically says: "You can add me to your project. *My* code will fulfill *your needs*. You won't have to write this code yourself. And that will make you very happy."

When I stumble upon a package that may provide the functionality that I need, the first thing I do is read the README file (and possibly any other documentation that is available). When the description of the package resembles my own ideas about the code that I was going to write if this package wouldn't exist, the next thing I do is dive into the code. I quickly scan the directory structure, the class names, then the code inside those classes, which I will then critically evaluate.

In the first place I look for the use cases that the package supports. The package maintainer has probably created this package to support one of their particular use cases. Most likely my own use case is (slightly if not vastly) different from theirs. So one particular characteristic I'm looking for is extensibility: is it possible to change the behavior of some of the classes in a package without actually modifying the code itself? Some good signs of extensibility are the use of interfaces and dependency injection.

Furthermore, the package's code probably contains bugs, which need to be fixed. While wading through the code, I try to estimate the amount of work needed to fix any problem with the code—does the package contain classes with too many responsibilities? Would it be possible to swap out faulty implementations by simply implementing an interface defined in the package, or would I be forced to copy long pages of code to replicate its behavior (after which I'll decide to drop the package anyway)?

Finally, I take a look at the automated tests that are available inside this package. Are there *enough* tests? Do they consist of clean code themselves? Do they make sense or are they just there for test coverage? What if there are no tests at all (which is the case for *many* packages out there)? How can I trust this code to work in my own project? How could I ever have the courage to put this code on a production server and let it be executed by real users?

The reason for my cautiousness when adding a dependency to my project is that once it's installed and I start using the code it contains, I become responsible for it.[10] Although many package maintainers are quite serious about delivering support for

---

[10]Igor Wiedler discusses this in detail in his article "Dependency Responsibility," https://igor.io/2013/09/24/dependency-responsibility.html

their packages, not every one of them will always fix any problem that gets reported, or add any feature that's missing, even if you're nice enough to create a pull request for it. Chances are you'll be on your own when the package doesn't meet your expectations.

So you need to be able to fix bugs, and add features to the package, without modifying the code inside the package (since you're not actually able to do so). You need to be comfortable with that.

What the Package Maintainer Needs to Do

As a package maintainer, you need to write code following established design principles, like the SOLID principles explained in the previous part of this book. But there are some other (much simpler) guidelines you should follow to produce good, or "clean," code.

Static Analysis

To verify that code quality has a certain level and doesn't degrade over time, you can leverage automated static analysis tools. These tools can inspect the code and bring out a verdict based on a set of rules that in most cases can be fully configured to reflect your own quality standards. Popular static analysis tools for PHP are PHPStan and so-called "inspections" in IDEs like JetBrains's PhpStorm. There are lots of other tools available though, most of which have been conveniently listed on a website called "PHP Quality Assurance".[11]

Add Tests

Of course it's important that your code looks good. But it's even more important that it runs well. And how would you be able to verify that? By adding an "appropriately sized" suite of tests to your package.

There are vastly different opinions about what this means exactly: how many tests should you write? Do you write the tests first[12] and later the code? Should you add integration tests or functional tests? What is the amount of code coverage your package needs?

---

[11]See also `https://phpqa.io/`

[12]Robert C. Martin discusses what a test-first approach means in his article "Test First," `https://8thlight.com/blog/uncle-bob/2013/09/23/Test-first.html`

The crucial question you should ask yourself is this: *do I care about the future of my code*? Tests are meant to allow for safe refactoring later on. If you just write the code and use it in one project then you may not feel the need to write tests for this code. On the contrary, you'd definitely need quite a large test suite if that code is going to be used *by anyone else* in *any other project*. In that case you want to keep fixing bugs or add new features to the package. If you have no tests, making those changes becomes difficult and dangerous. How can you trust the package to work as expected after you've made the changes?

So tests support refactoring. They will greatly help you prevent regressions in future commits. But tests also serve as the specification of your code. They describe the expected behavior when a user would do something with the code in some specific situation. This is why tests could in theory serve as documentation for the code.

This is not really true of course, because tests only tell little parts of the story, but never the whole story. They have no introduction, no epilogue, and they don't fill in any (conceptual) knowledge gaps. Nevertheless, tests as a specification of the code and a description of its behavior are important because they let users of the code know which method calls they can make, what kind of arguments they should provide, and which preconditions are required before they can do so.

If a package has no tests or too few tests, this is what it communicates to users: "I don't care about the future of this code. I'm not sure that, when I change something, everything will keep working. In fact, I give you no hope that this code is reliable at all. I use it today; I don't care about tomorrow."

Set Up Continuous Integration

All tests need to be run often. Of course, you run tests all the time while developing. But every time you create another branch (for a new version), patch branches with some bug fix, or when you accept pull requests, you would have to run the tests again. Otherwise you won't know for sure that everything works as expected. Doing all of this manually would be too much work. And this is where continuous integration comes in handy.

Continuous integration means that every change to a project's repository will trigger its build process. If anything goes wrong, the project team will receive a notification and they can (immediately) fix the problem.

For software products that will be shipped, a build process may include the creation of an executable, or a ZIP file. For most projects the build process is mainly interesting because all the tests will be run. Some other artifacts that may be produced by the build process are code coverage and code quality metrics.

Conclusion

Most of the things that we discussed in this chapter were of a very practical nature. The underlying reason for this was: you need to get the infrastructure of your package right, before you can make it reusable in the first place. For you, your teammates, or external developers from all over the world to be able to use your package in their projects, it needs to be *a really good product*. You (or the package maintainer succeeding you) need to be able to release the package once and to support future releases by means of a good infrastructure. Users should be able to understand what the package is all about, how they can use it, and what they can expect from you with regard to future versions.

Code being released as one package constitutes the first aspect of the *cohesion* of a package. If the *release* process of a package is unmanageable or not managed at all, it can not be properly *reused*. This chapter gave you an overview of what it means for a package to be released in a manageable way, from the first release, to any future release, and from patch versions to major versions. There are many details to this process that we didn't cover here, but those are often specific for the programming language that you use.

One last remark before we continue to discuss the second cohesion principle, the *Common Reuse* principle. It's possible that I have scared you, writing about all these things that you need to do to create "good" packages. Maybe you are tempted to put this book down and to let go of your dream to one day publish a package that is used by many, many people. But don't give up! Of course, creating your first package might give you some trouble. It will take some time, you may feel a bit insecure about the steps you take, you may forget some things, you may make some mistakes. The good thing is that you will learn quickly, develop some kind of habit, and in my experience other people are not shy about giving you useful feedback on your packages, which should help you release even better packages over time.

After you finish reading this book, go ahead and look for some practical suggestions to do the things that were described in a more abstract way in this chapter, and become part of the lively, code-sharing community of developers.

CHAPTER 7

The Common Reuse Principle

In Chapter 6, we discussed the *Release/Reuse Equivalence* principle. It's the first principle of package cohesion: it tells an important part of the story about which classes belong together in a package, namely those that you can properly release and maintain as a package. You need to take care of delivering a package that is a true product.

If you follow all the advice given in the previous chapter, you will have a well-behaving package. It has great usability and it's easily available, so it will be quickly adopted by other developers. But even when a package behaves well *as a package*, it may at the same time not be very *useful*.

Let's say you have a nice collection of very useful classes, implementing several interesting features. When you group those classes into packages, there are two extremes that need to be avoided. If you release all the classes as one package, you force your users to pull the entire package into their project, even if they use just a very small part of it. This is quite a maintenance burden for them.

On the other hand, if you put every single class in a separate package, you will have to release a lot of packages. This increases your own maintenance burden. At the same time, users have a hard time managing their own list of dependencies and keeping track of all the new versions of those tiny packages.

In this chapter, we discuss the second package cohesion principle, which is called the *Common Reuse* principle. It helps you decide which classes should be put together in a package, and what's more important, which classes should be moved to another package. When we're selecting classes or interfaces for reuse, the *Common Reuse* principle tells us that[1]:

> *Classes that are used together are packaged together.*

---

[1]Robert C. Martin, "The principles of OOD," http://butunclebob.com/ArticleS.UncleBob.PrinciplesOfOod

© Matthias Noback 2018
M. Noback, *Principles of Package Design*, https://doi.org/10.1007/978-1-4842-4119-6_7

So when you design a package you should put classes in it that are going to be used *together*. This may seem a bit obvious; you wouldn't put completely unrelated classes that are *never* used together in one package. But things become somewhat less obvious when we consider the other side of this principle—you should not put classes in a package that are *not* used together. This includes classes that are *likely not* to be used together (which leaves the user with irrelevant code imported into their project).

In this chapter, we look at some packages that obviously violate this rule: they contain all sorts of classes that are not used together—either because those classes implement isolated features or because they have different dependencies. Sometimes the package maintainer puts those classes in the same package because they have some conceptual similarity. Some may think it enhances the usability of the package for them or its users.

At the end of this chapter, we try to formulate the principle in a more positive way and we discuss some guiding questions that can be used to make your packages conform to the *Common Reuse* principle.

There are many signs, or "smells," by which you can recognize a package that violates the *Common Reuse* principle. I'll discuss some of these signs, using some real-world packages as examples. A quick word before we continue—in no way do I want to dispute the greatness of these packages. They are well-established packages, created by expert developers, and used by many people all over the world. However, I don't agree with some of the package design choices that were made. So you should take my comments not as angry criticism, but as a gesture toward what I think is the ideal package design approach.

Feature Strata

The most important characteristic of packages that violate the *Common Reuse* principle is what I call "strata of features". I really like the term *strata*, and this is the perfect time to use it. A *stratum* is:

> *A layer of material, naturally or artificially formed, often one of a number of parallel layers, one upon another.*[2]

I'd like to define "feature strata" as features existing together in the same package, but not dependent on each other. This means that you would be able to use feature A

---

[2]https://www.dictionary.com/browse/strata

without feature B, but adding feature B is possible without disturbing feature A. It also means that afterward, disabling feature B is no problem and won't cause feature A to break. Feature A and B don't touch; they work in *parallel*.

In the context of packages, feature strata often manifest themselves as classes that belong together because they implement some specific feature. But then after one feature has been implemented, the maintainer of the package kept adding new features, consisting of conglomerates of classes to the same package. In most cases, this happens because the features are *conceptually*, but not *materially*, related.

Obvious Stratification

Sometimes you can recognize a stratified package by the fact that it literally contains a different namespace for each *feature stratum*. There are many examples of this, but let's take a look at the symfony/security package,[3] which contains the Symfony Security component.[4] As you can see by looking at its directory/namespace tree, it has four major namespaces—Acl, Core, Csrf, and Http—each of them containing many classes (see Listing 7-1).

Listing 7-1. The Directory Tree of the symfony/security Package

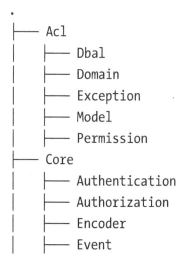

```
.
├── Acl
│   ├── Dbal
│   ├── Domain
│   ├── Exception
│   ├── Model
│   ├── Permission
├── Core
│   ├── Authentication
│   ├── Authorization
│   ├── Encoder
│   ├── Event
```

---

[3]https://packagist.org/packages/symfony/security
[4]https://github.com/symfony/Security

```
|       ├── Exception
|       ├── Role
|       ├── User
|       ├── Util
|       └── Validator
├── Csrf
└── Http
```

Classes from these major namespaces don't have to be used together at the same time: classes in `Acl` only depend on `Core`, classes in `Http` depend on classes in `Core` and optionally on classes in `Csrf`. Not the other way around. This means that if someone were to install this package to use the `Csrf` classes, they would only use a small subset of this package. So if we think about what the *Common Reuse* principle was all about ("Classes that are used together are packaged together"), then this is a clear violation of this principle.

As you can see, some of the major namespaces are split up into minor namespaces. And as it turns out, many of the classes from the minor namespaces can be used separately from classes in the other namespaces. This again indicates that the *Common Reuse* principle has been violated, and that the package should be split. Fortunately, the package maintainers already decided to split this package into several other packages, so now at least the major namespaces have their own package definition file and can be installed separately.

Obfuscated Stratification

In many other cases, a package has feature strata that aren't so easy to spot. The classes that are grouped around a certain functionality are not separated by their namespace, but by some other principle of division, for instance by the *type* of the class. Take a look at the `nelmio/security-bundle` package,[5] which contains `NelmioSecurityBundle`,[6] which can be used in Symfony projects to add some specific security measures that are not provided by the framework itself. Because of the nature of the Symfony `HttpKernel`,[7]

---

[5]https://packagist.org/packages/nelmio/security-bundle
[6]https://github.com/nelmio/NelmioSecurityBundle
[7]https://github.com/symfony/HttpKernel

everything related to security can be implemented as an event listener, which hooks into the process of converting a request to a response. Some security-related event listeners will prevent the kernel from further handling the current request (for instance, based on the protocol used), and some listeners modify the final response (e.g., encrypt cookies or session data).

By looking at the directory tree of this package, you can easily recognize the fact that most of the features are introduced as event listeners, some of which may use utility classes like Encrypter and Signer (see Listing 7-2).

Listing 7-2. The Directory Structure of the nelmio/security-bundle Package

```
.
├── ContentSecurityPolicy
│   └── ContentSecurityPolicyParser.php
├── Encrypter.php
├── EventListener
│   ├── ClickjackingListener.php
│   ├── ContentSecurityPolicyListener.php
│   ├── EncryptedCookieListener.php
│   ├── ExternalRedirectListener.php
│   ├── FlexibleSslListener.php
│   ├── ForcedSslListener.php
│   └── SignedCookieListener.php
├── Session
│   └── CookieSessionHandler.php
└── Signer.php
```

As you could've guessed by the names of the listeners, each listener has a particular functionality and each of the listeners can be used *separately*. This guess can be confirmed by looking at the available configuration options for this package (see Listing 7-3).

Listing 7-3. The Available Configuration Options for the nelmio/security-bundle Package

```
nelmio_security:
    # signs/verifies all cookies
    signed_cookie:
        names: ['*']
```

```
# encrypt all cookies
encrypted_cookie:
    names: ['*']

# prevents framing of the entire site
clickjacking:
    paths:
        '^/.*': DENY

# prevents redirections outside the website's domain
external_redirects:
    abort: true
    log: true

# prevents inline scripts, unsafe eval, external
# scripts/images/styles/frames, etc
csp:
    default: [ self ]

...
```

It becomes clear that all of these listeners represent a different functionality that can be configured on its own and any of the listeners can be disabled, while the other one will still keep working. This forces us to conclude that when you use one class from this package, you will not always use all the other (nor even most of the other) classes inside this package. And thus, the package violates the *Common Reuse* principle in a very clear way. Somebody who wants to use only one of the features provided by this bundle (and they can!) still has to install the entire bundle.

It becomes slightly more interesting when we look at the remaining configuration options, where it appears that some parts of this package are even mutually exclusive: HTTPS handling can not be "forced" and "flexible" at the same time (see Listing 7-4).

Listing 7-4. HTTPS Handling Can't Be Configured to be "Forced" and "Flexible" at the Same Time

```
nelmio_security:
    ...
```

```
   # forced HTTPS handling, don't combine with flexible mode
   # and make sure you have SSL working on your site before
   # enabling this
#    forced_ssl:
#        hsts_max_age: 2592000 # 30 days
#        hsts_subdomains: true

   # flexible HTTPS handling
#    flexible_ssl:
#        cookie_name: auth
#        unsecured_logout: false
```

This means that when you use one particular class in this package, i.e. the ForcedSslListener, you will definitely not use *all* other classes of this package. In fact, you will *with certainty* not use FlexibleSslListener. Of course, this definitely asks for a package split, so users would not have to be concerned with this exclusiveness.

Classes That Can Only Be Used When ... Is Installed

It should be noted that the previous examples were about packages that provide *separate* feature strata, but each of those features has the *same dependencies* (in this case, other Symfony components or the entire Symfony framework). The following examples will be about feature strata within packages that have different dependencies themselves.

Let's take a look at the monolog/monolog package,[8] which contains the Monolog logger.[9] The primary class of this package is the Logger class (obviously). However, the real handling of log messages is done by instances of HandlerInterface. By combining different handlers, activation strategies, formatters, and processors, every part of logging messages can be configured. The package tries to offer support for anything you can write log messages to, like a file, a logging server, a database, etc. This results in the list of files in Listing 7-5 (it's quite big and still it's shorter than the real list).

---

[8]https://packagist.org/packages/monolog/monolog
[9]https://github.com/Seldaek/monolog

Listing 7-5. List of Files in the monolog/monolog Package (Abbreviated)

```
.
├── Formatter
│       ├── ChromePHPFormatter.php
│       ├── FormatterInterface.php
│       ├── GelfMessageFormatter.php
│       ├── JsonFormatter.php
│       ├── LogstashFormatter.php
│       └── WildfireFormatter.php
├── Handler
│       ├── AmqpHandler.php
│       ├── BufferHandler.php
│       ├── ChromePHPHandler.php
│       ├── CouchDBHandler.php
│       ├── CubeHandler.php
│       ├── DoctrineCouchDBHandler.php
│       ├── ErrorLogHandler.php
│       ├── FingersCrossedHandler.php
│       ├── FirePHPHandler.php
│       ├── GelfHandler.php
│       ├── HandlerInterface.php
│       ├── HipChatHandler.php
│       ├── MailHandler.php
│       ├── MongoDBHandler.php
│       ├── NativeMailerHandler.php
│       ├── NewRelicHandler.php
│       ├── NullHandler.php
│       ├── PushoverHandler.php
│       ├── RavenHandler.php
│       ├── RedisHandler.php
│       ├── RotatingFileHandler.php
│       ├── SocketHandler.php
│       ├── StreamHandler.php
│       ├── SwiftMailerHandler.php
│       ├── SyslogHandler.php
```

```
|     ├── TestHandler.php
|     └── ZendMonitorHandler.php
├── Logger.php
└── Processor
      ├── MemoryProcessor.php
      ├── ProcessIdProcessor.php
      └── PsrLogMessageProcessor.php
```

A developer can install this package and start instantiating handler classes for any storage facility that is *already available in their development environment.* As a user you don't need to think about which package you should install; it's always the main package. This would seem to have a high usability factor: isn't this easy? Whatever your situation is, just install the monolog/monolog package and you can use it right away (this is known as the "batteries included" approach).

As we will see, this design choice complicates things a lot, for the user as well as for the package maintainer. The thing is, this package isn't entirely honest about its dependencies. It contains code for all kinds of things, but all this code needs many different extra things to be able to function correctly. For instance, the MongoDBHandler needs the mongo PHP extension to be installed. Now when I install monolog/monolog, the package manager won't verify that the extension is installed, because it's listed as an *optional* dependency (ext-mongo under the suggest key) in the package definition file (see Listing 7-6).

Listing 7-6. Optional Dependencies for the monolog/monolog Package

```
{
  "name": "monolog/monolog",
  ...
  "require": {
    "php": ">=5.3.0",
    "psr/log": "~1.0"
  },
  ...
  "suggest": {
    "mlehner/gelf-php": "Send log messages to GrayLog2",
    "raven/raven": "Send log messages to Sentry",
    "doctrine/couchdb": "Send log messages to CouchDB",
```

```
   "ext-mongo": "Send log messages to MongoDB",
   "aws/aws-sdk-php": "Send log messages to AWS services"
   ...
 },
 ...
}
```

Why didn't the maintainer of monolog/monolog add the ext-mongo dependency to the list of required packages? Well, imagine a developer who only wants to use the StreamHandler, which just appends log messages to a file on the local filesystem. They don't need a Mongo database nor the mongo extension to be available. If ext-mongo would be a required dependency, installing the monolog/monolog package would force them to also install the mongo extension, even though the code that really needs the extension will never be executed in their environment. This is why ext-mongo is just a *suggested dependency*.

So if I want to use its MongoDBHandler for storing my log messages in a Mongo database, I have to *manually* add ext-mongo as a dependency to my own project (as is shown in Listing 7-7). This will make the package manager check if the mongo extension has indeed been installed.

Listing 7-7. Manually Adding ext-mongo as a Project Dependency

```
{
    "require": {
        "ext-mongo": ...
    }
}
```

The first issue for me is that I don't know which version of the mongo PHP extension I need to install to be able to use the MongoDBHandler. There's no way to find that out, other than to just try installing the latest stable version and *hope* that it's supported by MongoDBHandler. I will only know this for sure if the MongoDBHandler comes with tests that fully specify its behavior. Then I could run the tests and see if they pass with the specific version of ext-mongo that I just installed. This is my first objection to the design choice of making the MongoDBHandler part of the core Monolog package.

The second objection to this approach is that it forces me to add the `mongo` extension to the list of dependencies *of my own project*. This is wrong, since it's not a dependency of *my* project but of the `monolog/monolog` package. It's a dependency of a *class inside that package*. My own project might not contain any code related to MongoDB at all, yet I have to require the `mongo` extension in my project because I want to use the `MongoDBHandler` class.

So the `monolog/monolog` package doesn't handle its dependencies well, and I have to do this myself. But this doesn't really match with the idea of a package manager, which I instruct to install each of my own dependencies and any dependencies required by these dependencies. I want all the packages I install to *fully take care of their own dependencies*. It's not my responsibility to know the dependencies of each class inside a package and to guess which ones I need to manually install to be able to use them. Furthermore, I should not be the one who needs to find out which version of a dependency is compatible with the code in the package. This is the task of the package maintainer.

This reasoning applies to each of the specific handlers that the `monolog/monolog` package supplies. And nearly all handlers will be used exclusively by any particular user, which means that the package violates the *Common Reuse* principle an equal number of times. For any handler in the package, the other handlers and their optional dependencies will probably never be used at the same time.

Suggested Refactoring

The solution to this problem is easy—split the `monolog/monolog` package. Each handler should have its own package, with its own *true* dependencies. For example, the `MongoDBHandler` would be in the `monolog/mongo-db-handler` package, which can be defined as in Listing 7-8.

Listing 7-8. The Definition File for the monolog/mongo-db-handler Package

```
{
    "name": "monolog/mongo-db-handler",
    "require": {
        "php": ">=5.3.2",
        "monolog/monolog": "~1.6"
        "ext-mongo": ">=1.2.12,<1.6-dev"
    }
}
```

This way, each specific handler package can be explicit about its dependencies and the supported versions of those dependencies too, and there are no optional dependencies anymore (think about it: how can a dependency be "optional" really?). If I choose to install the monolog/mongo-db-handler, I can rest assured that every dependency will be checked for me and that after installing the package, every line of code inside it is executable in my development environment. Figure 7-1 shows what the dependency hierarchy looks like after this change.

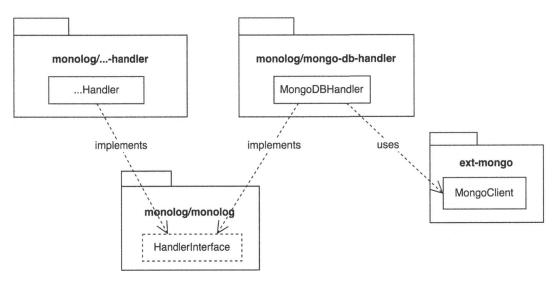

Figure 7-1. *monolog packages with explicit dependencies*

Previously, the package definition file of monolog/monolog contained some useful suggestions as to what other extensions and packages the user could install to unlock some of its features. Now that the ext-mongo dependency was moved to the monolog/ mongo-db-handler package, how does a user know they can use a Mongo database to store log messages? Well, this monolog/mongo-db-handler package itself could be listed under the suggested dependencies for the monolog/monolog package, as shown in Listing 7-9.

Listing 7-9. Suggested Dependencies for the monolog/monolog Package

```
{
  "name": "monolog/monolog",
  ...
```

```
  "suggest": {
    "monolog/mongo-db-handler": "Send log messages to MongoDB",
    "monolog/gelf-handler": "Send log messages to GrayLog2",
    "monolog/raven-handler": "Send log messages to Sentry",
    ...
  },
  ...
}
```

A Package Should Be "Linkable"

Let's take one last look at `MongoDBHandler`, as it's currently still a part of the `monolog/monolog` package. We already concluded that after installing the package, you would not be able to use this class without also installing the `mongo` PHP extension first. If we don't do this, and we try to use this specific handler, we would get all kinds of errors, in particular errors related to classes that were not found. The code inside the `MongoDBHandler` is syntactically correct, it just doesn't work in the context of this project.

We need to make a conceptual division here when it comes to correctness, a division that is not often made by PHP developers. In many programming languages, problems with the code can occur at *compile* time or at *link* time. Compiling code means checking its syntax, building an abstract syntax tree, and converting the higher-level code to lower-level code. The result of the compile step are object files, which need to be linked together, in order to be executable. During the link process, references to classes and functions will be verified. If a function or class is not defined in any of the object files, the linker produces an error.

One of the characteristics of PHP is that it has no link process. It compiles code, yes, but if a class or a function does not exist, it will only be noticed at runtime, and even then in most cases, at the very last moment.

I strongly believe that even though PHP allows us to be very flexible in this regard, we must teach ourselves to think more in a "compiled language" way. We have to ask ourselves: would this code compile? It should, definitely, otherwise it would just be malformed code. And regarding every explicit, non-optional dependency of my package: would this code "link"? The answer would be "No" if the `MongoDBHandler` stays inside the `monolog/monolog` package, which has the `mongo` extension as a suggested dependency only. If we move the `MongoDBHandler` to its own `monolog/mongo-db-handler` package, which has an explicit dependency on `ext-mongo`, the answer will be "Yes," as it should be.

STATIC ANALYSIS TOOLS AS SUBSTITUTES FOR A REAL COMPILER

Over the last few years, PHP as a programming language has moved further and further into the direction of being a statically typed language. PHP code will remain a dynamic language with compilation at runtime. But the language has better type checking with every release. Besides, PHP developers compensate for what the language doesn't offer by using all kinds of static analysis tools. These tools become more and more popular, since they help catch a lot of potential issues with the code, before the code runs on some server.

In the context of our discussion about compiling and linking, PHPStan deserves a first mention here:

> *PHPStan moves PHP closer to compiled languages in the sense that the correctness of each line of the code can be checked before you run the actual line.*[10]

Comparable tools are Psalm[11] and Phan.[12]

There's another tool worth mentioning here. It's called Composer Require Checker[13] and it checks whether a package uses imported symbols (classes, interfaces, etc.) that aren't part of its direct dependencies. This is very useful, since it will prevent the scenario where your package uses a class that's inside a package that is only *indirectly* a dependency of your package. In other words, if Package A depends on Package B and B depends on C, then if A also depends on C, it needs to make this dependency explicit. Otherwise, if one day B stops depending on C, this will break A. If you use PhpStorm as your IDE, the PHP Inspections plugin can also tell you about implicit dependencies.

Cleaner Releases

There's one more characteristic of the `monolog/monolog` package that I'd like to discuss here, which again points us in the direction of creating separate packages for each of the specific handlers.

---

[10]https://github.com/phpstan/phpstan

[11]https://github.com/vimeo/psalm

[12]https://github.com/phan/phan

[13]https://github.com/maglnet/ComposerRequireChecker

As we saw in the chapter about the *Release/Reuse Equivalence* principle, it's important for a package to be a good software product. One of the important characteristics of good software is that new versions don't cause backward compatibility breaks. However, the `MongoDBHandler` in the `monolog/monolog` package shows clear signs of a struggle for backward compatibility (see Listing 7-10).

Listing 7-10. The MongoDBHandler

```php
class MongoDBHandler extends AbstractProcessingHandler
{
    // ...

    public function __construct(
        $mongo,
        $database,
        $collection,
        ...
    ) {
        if (!($mongo instanceof MongoClient
            || $mongo instanceof Mongo)) {
            throw new InvalidArgumentException('...');
        }

        // ...
    }

    // ...
}
```

The first constructor parameter $mongo has no explicit type. Instead, the validity of the argument is being checked inside the constructor and this validation step allows us to use two different kinds of $mongo objects. It should be either an instance of MongoClient or an instance of Mongo. Both are classes from the mongo PHP extension, but the Mongo class is deprecated since version 1.3.0 of the extension.

So now there's an ugly if clause inside the constructor of this class, which prevents the $mongo argument from being strictly typed, even if I have the latest version of the mongo extension installed in my environment. This shouldn't be necessary. I'd like the handler to look like the one in Listing 7-11 instead.

Listing 7-11. The MongoDBHandler with a Strictly Typed Constructor Argument

```
class MongoDBHandler extends AbstractProcessingHandler
{
    ...

    public function __construct(
        MongoClient $mongo,
        $database,
        ...
    ) {
        // no need for extra validation

        // ...
    }

    // ...
}
```

But if we remove the if clause, this class would be useless for people who have an older version of mongo installed on their system.

The only way to solve this dilemma is to create extra branches in the version control repository of the monolog/monolog package—a branch for version ranges of MongoDB that should receive special treatment, e.g. monolog/monolog@mongo_db_older_than_1_3_0 and monolog/monolog@mongo_db. Of course, this will soon end in a big mess. The monolog/monolog package has many more handlers that may require such treatment.

Let's fast-forward to the already suggested solution of moving the MongoDBHandler to its own package, the definition file of which looks like the one in Listing 7-12.

Listing 7-12. The Definition File for the monolog/mongo-db-handler Package (Revisited)

```
{
    "name": "monolog/mongo-db-handler",
    "require": {
        "php": ">=5.3.2",
```

```
        "monolog/monolog": "~1.6"
        "ext-mongo": ">=1.2.12,<1.6-dev"
    }
}
```

This `monolog/mongo-db-handler` package is hosted inside a separate repository, so it doesn't need to keep up with the versions of the core `monolog/monolog` package. This means it's possible to add branches corresponding to different versions of the `mongo` extension. For instance, you could have a 1.2.x branch and a 1.3.x branch, corresponding to the version of the `mongo` extension that is supported. Then someone who has version 1.2 of the `mongo` extension installed could add version 1.2 of `monolog/monolog-db-handler` as a dependency to their project (see Listing 7-13).

Listing 7-13. Adding Version 1.2 of monolog/monolog-db-handler as a Dependency

```
{
    "require": {
        "monolog/monolog-db-handler": "1.2.*"
    }
}
```

Someone who already has the latest version of the `mongo` extension would simply choose `"~1.3"` as the version constraint.

Splitting the package based on its (optional) dependencies is advantageous not only to the user of the package. It will also help the maintainer a lot. They can let someone else maintain the MongoDB-specific handler package, someone who already keeps a close eye on the `mongo` extension releases. This person doesn't have to be able to modify the main `monolog/monolog` package. This package automatically becomes a more stable package, because it has fewer reasons to change (see also Chapter 8 about the *Common Closure* principle). This is by itself a good thing for its users, who don't need to keep track of every new version that is released because of a change in one of the handlers they don't use.

THE COST OF SPLITTING

When discussing the package design principles and applying them to real-world packages, the advice is usually to split the package into smaller ones. While we're still in the middle of discussing all the reasons for doing so, it's good to mention that there's a trade-off involved in splitting packages. The smaller your packages are, the more you will have of them, the more work you have to put into making new releases, managing the repositories, their issues and pull requests, etc. The larger your packages are, the more complicated they are to work with from a user perspective. The package will need to be upgraded often, and the user will pull in lots of code and lots of dependencies they don't need.

It's good to keep this in mind when you're a package developer. You need to find that golden middle between too many small packages, and too few large packages.

A technical solution that could be helpful is the so-called "mono-repo". It means that the code for all your packages will be hosted in one repository. Any change to any of the packages will be committed to that repository. To make it possible for users to install every package separately, there will be a read-only repository for each of the subpackages inside the mono-repo. These sub-repositories will be updated upon every change to the main repository. For Git, this process is called "subtree split". There's no need to manually set it up, since there are automated solutions, like Git Subtree Split as a Service.[14]

Bonus Features

We've looked at obvious and non-obvious feature strata and why these are characteristics of packages that violate the *Common Reuse* principle. Sometimes features are not really strata, but single classes that nevertheless don't belong inside a package. Let's take a look at the `matthiasnoback/microsoft-translator` package[15] I created myself. This package contains the MicrosoftTranslator library,[16] which can

---

[14]https://www.subtreesplit.com/

[15]https://packagist.org/packages/matthiasnoback/microsoft-translator

[16]https://github.com/matthiasnoback/microsoft-translator

be used for translating text using the Microsoft (Bing) Translator API. The translator depends on the kriswallsmith/buzz package,[17] which itself contains an HTTP client called Buzz.[18] My package uses its Browser class to make HTTP requests to the Microsoft OAuth and Translator APIs, as you may guess by its (stripped) directory structure (see Listing 7-14).

Listing 7-14. The Abbreviated Directory Structure of the matthiasnoback/ microsoft-translator Package

```
.
├── Buzz
├── Exception
├── MicrosoftOAuth
└── MicrosoftTranslator
```

While I was developing this library, I realized that my application might make many duplicate calls to the Microsoft Translator API. For instance, it would ask the translation service several times to translate the word "Submit" to Dutch. And even though this would trigger a new HTTP request every time, the response from the API would always be the same. In order to prevent these duplicate requests, I decided to add a caching layer to the package and I thought it would be a good idea to do this by wrapping the Buzz browser client in a CachedClient[19] class. The CachedClient class would analyze each incoming request and look in the cache to see if it had made this request before. If so, the cached response would be returned; otherwise, the request would be forwarded to the real Buzz client, and afterwards the fresh response would be stored in the cache.

See Figure 7-2 for the dependency diagram of the microsoft-translator package.

---

[17]https://packagist.org/packages/kriswallsmith/buzz

[18]https://github.com/kriswallsmith/Buzz

[19]https://github.com/matthiasnoback/microsoft-translator/blob/v0.6.1/src/
MatthiasNoback/Buzz/Client/CachedClient.php

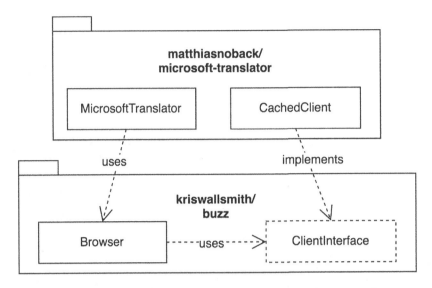

Figure 7-2. *Dependency diagram of the microsoft-translator package*

Though at the time I thought the design of this library was pretty good, I would now try to eliminate the dependency on Buzz. There's nothing so special about Buzz that this package would *really* need it. In fact, all it needs is "some HTTP client". Considering the need for abstraction, I would introduce an interface for HTTP clients (e.g., HttpClientInterface) and then create a separate package, called matthiasnoback/microsoft-translator-buzz, which would provide an implementation of my own HttpClientInterface that uses Buzz. Even better, I could rely on an existing abstraction for HTTP clients (e.g., HTTPlug[20]) or some otherwise standardized and widely supported interface, like the upcoming PHP Standards Recommendation (PSR) 18.[21]

But there's some other thing that's wrong with the design of this library: it contains this smart little CachedClient class. Since it's indeed such a useful class, every user of this package will likely use this CachedClient class together with the other classes in the package. So there's no immediate violation of the *Common Reuse* principle here. However, suppose that your project already depends on the kriswallsmith/buzz

---

[20]https://github.com/php-http/httplug
[21]https://www.php-fig.org/psr/

package and you need a cache implementation for the Buzz browser client. The matthiasnoback/microsoft-translator package contains such an implementation, so you would simply install it and use only its CachedClient class, and no other class from the same package. Now this makes it crystal-clear that the package does indeed violate the *Common Reuse* principle. If you use a class from this package, you will not use *all* the other classes.

Suggested Refactoring

As you may have guessed, the solution to this problem would be to extract the CachedClient class and put it in another package, matthiasnoback/cached-buzz-client, which has nothing to do with the Microsoft Translator and just depends on kriswallsmith/buzz. That way, anybody can install just this package in their project and use the cache layer for Buzz clients. Even better, this package could evolve separately from the microsoft-translator package. Other people may contribute to it by adding features or fixing bugs. These enhancements would become available for everyone who depends on the cached-buzz-client package. When installing the microsoft-translator package, the cached-buzz-client package could be a suggested, optional dependency (see Figure 7-3).

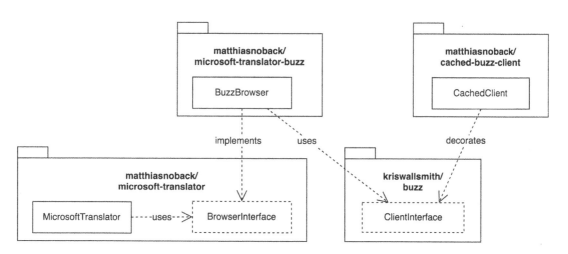

Figure 7-3. *Dependency diagram of the microsoft-translator package after moving the CachedClient class out*

It's really great that Buzz now has a way to cache HTTP responses, and this could indeed be interesting functionality for other people. However, if we would have thought more carefully before jumping in and extending the Buzz HTTP client itself, we could have realized that a much simpler solution was just around the corner. Rephrasing the functional requirements as "to be able to cache translation results," all we need is to extend the functionality of the translator class itself. We could do so using the previously demonstrated technique of class decoration using composition. First, we need an interface for the translator class. Then we create a new class that implements that interface *and* receives an instance of that interface as a constructor argument. See Listing 7-15 for the result. The demonstrated technique of caching a function's return value is called "memoization".

Listing 7-15. Wrapping the Translator and Caching Return Values of the translate() Method

```
interface TranslatorInterface
{
    public function translate(string $text, string $to): string;
}

final class MicrosoftTranslator implements TranslatorInterface
{
    public function translate(string $text, string $to): string
    {
        // make a call to the remote web service
    }
}

final class CachedTranslator implements TranslatorInterface
{
    private $results = [];

    public function __construct(TranslatorInterface $translator)
    {
        $this->translator = $translator;
    }
```

```php
    public function translate(string $text, string $to): string
    {
        if (!isset($this->results[$text][$to])) {
            $result = $this->translator
                            ->translate($text, $to);

            $this->results[$text][$to] = $result;
        }

        return $this->results[$text][$to];
    }
}

$translator = new CachedTranslator(new MicrosoftTranslator());

// this call will hit the remote service:
$translator->translate('Submit', 'nl');

// the next call will use the cached result:
$translator->translate('Submit', 'nl');
```

The CachedClient class we just discussed was a nice example of a "bonus feature" that consists of only a single class. It seems overkill to install an entire package with many classes in your project, just to use one class. But of course, this is a sliding scale. Which number or percentage of classes would be acceptable for a package to remain intact and not be split into multiple other packages?

Guiding Questions

These questions help you decide for each class whether or not it should be in the package you're working on. In practice I tend to just create the class inside the package I'm already working on. Afterward, I may decide to move it to another package, based on the following guiding questions:

- *Does the class introduce a dependency?*

    If it does, is it an optional/suggested dependency? Then you have to create a new package containing this class, explicitly mentioning its dependency.

167

- *Would the class be useful without the rest of the package?*

  If it would, then you have to create a new package to enable users
  to pull in only the code they want to use.

Asking yourself these two questions, and following the advice they give, will automatically divide your packages according to their dependencies and the functionality they provide. These aspects are also the main reasons why people will select a certain package and not another one—whether or not it introduces too much or too little of the functionality they need, and whether or not its dependencies are compatible with the dependencies of their own projects. If either of these aspects don't match with the requirements of the user, they won't install the package.

When to Apply the Principle

You can apply the *Common Reuse* principle at different moments in the package development lifecycle, for instance when you're creating a new package for existing classes. The first thing you will need to do is group the classes that are *always used together* and put them in a package. When you need class A and *it always needs* class B, it would be a bad idea to put these classes in different packages, `package-a` and `package-b`. Separating these classes would require a developer who would like to use class A to install both `package-a` and `package-b`.

But the *Common Reuse* principle should also constantly be applied when you're adding new classes to an existing package. You need to check if the new class you're about to add will *always* be used together with all the other classes in the package. Chances are that by adding a new class to a package you're adding features to the package that aren't used by everybody who would require the package as a dependency of their project.

When to Violate the Principle

As we see in the next chapter, the *Common Reuse* principle is a principle that can only be maximized. You cannot *always* follow it perfectly. There are times when you may choose to put two classes in one package that *can* be used separately. Strictly speaking, you would thereby violate the principle, but there may be good reasons to do so. First of all, for convenience. Every package you create needs some extra care. It requires time and energy from you as the package maintainer and there's a limit to how many packages you can or want to maintain.

Another reason to violate the principle is that you may know all about your target audience. When you know that almost all of the developers who use your package are using it inside a project built using the Laravel framework, you can follow the *Common Reuse* principle less strictly and add some classes to your package, which may only make sense when someone uses the full-stack Laravel framework. These classes would normally belong in a separate package because they could in theory be used separately, but in practice they will always be used together, which allows you to put them in the same package.

Why Not to Violate the Principle

In most cases, however, there's the following good reason to *not* violate the *Common Reuse* principle: every class that's part of your package is *susceptible to change*. Maybe one of its methods contains a bug, or some of its functionality needs to be changed. Maybe its interface needs to be modified and a backward compatibility break will be introduced. As a user of the package, you need to follow all the changes and decide if and when to upgrade to a new version. This takes time, because after upgrading a package, you need to check all the parts of your project that use classes from the package. Maybe you have some automated tests for this, maybe not.

However, you can't choose *not* to upgrade. You need to take care that your project depends on the latest stable versions of all packages, to prevent (future) problems like depending on deprecated or even abandoned packages. If the package you depend on is big, contains lots of classes, and is related to all kinds of things, upgrading it will be quite a problem. There are many points of contact between the code in your project and the code inside the package, which means that changes will have many side effects.

On the contrary, when the package you depend on is small, it will be easier to track the changes and less painful to upgrade the package. There will be fewer points of contact, and the chance that an upgrade will break your project is consequently much smaller.

So you greatly help the users of your package when you keep your package small and only put classes in it that they will actually use. Then they will be able to upgrade their dependencies fearlessly.

Conclusion

We have found out many things about the *Common Reuse* principle and by now it should be clear that there are some good reasons for splitting packages. Those reasons have advantages for both users and maintainers. A package that adheres to the *Common Reuse* principle has the following characteristics:

- It's coherent: All the classes it contains are about the same thing. Users don't need to install a large package just to use one class or a small group of classes.

- It has no "optional" dependencies: all its dependencies are true requirements; they are mentioned explicitly and have sensible version ranges. Users don't need to manually add extra dependencies to their project.

- They use dependency inversion to make dependencies abstract instead of concrete.

- As an effect, they are open for extension and closed for modification. Adding or modifying an alternative implementation doesn't mean opening the package, but creating an extra package.

CHAPTER 8

The Common Closure Principle

In the previous chapter, we discussed the *Common Reuse* principle. It was the second principle of package cohesion and it told us that we should put classes in a package that will be used together with the other classes in the package. If a user wants to use a class or a group of classes separately, this calls for a package split.

The third principle of package cohesion is called the *Common Closure* principle. It's closely related to the *Common Reuse* principle because it gives you another perspective on *granularity*: you will get another answer on the question as to which classes belong together in a package and which don't. The principle says that[1]:

> *The classes in a package should be closed together against the same kinds of changes. A change that affects a package affects all the classes in that package.*

So "common closure" actually means *being closed* against the same kinds of changes. With regard to the code in a package, this means that when something needs to change, it's likely that the change that is requested will affect *only one* package. Also, when a requirement changes and it affects one package, it will likely affect *all* classes inside that package.

The primary justification for this principle is that we want change to be limited to the smallest number of packages possible. People who have added your package as a dependency to their project will likely keep track of new releases of that package, to keep all the code in their project up-to-date. When a new version of the package becomes available, the user will upgrade their project to require the new version. But they only

---

[1]Robert C. Martin, Engineering Notebook, C++ Report, Nov-Dec, 1996 (PDF available on `http://butunclebob.com/ArticleS.UncleBob.PrinciplesOfOod`).

© Matthias Noback 2018
M. Noback, *Principles of Package Design*, https://doi.org/10.1007/978-1-4842-4119-6_8

want to do so if the changes *you* made to the package have something to do with the way the package is used in *their* project, since every upgrade requires them to verify that their code still works correctly with the new version of your package.

As a package maintainer, you should follow the *Common Closure* principle to prevent yourself from "opening" a package for all kinds of unrelated reasons. It helps you prevent bringing out new releases that are irrelevant to most of your users. With this goal in mind, the principle advises you to put classes in different packages if they have different reasons to change.

These reasons can be divided into several types, each of which we discuss in the following sections.

A Change in One of the Dependencies

Consider a package that still uses the deprecated PHP `mysql_*` functions for interaction with a MySQL database. You decide that you want to remove all occurrences of these functions in the package and instead use the much better alternative, PDO[2]. You start working on this, but it soon becomes clear that *of all the classes* inside the package, only two classes need to be modified. This would normally be a good thing, but in the context of package design, it means that the package violates the *Common Closure* principle—the files inside the package are not all closed against the same kinds of changes. Only some classes are affected by the recently changed requirements, while many classes are not. In other words, most classes are closed against a change related to database management, while some are not.

The classes that were changed together should have been in a separate package. This package would contain all the classes that will together be affected by the same kinds of changes. It would contain classes responsible for communicating with a MySQL database. The other packages would contain the remaining classes, which have nothing to do with the concrete way in which a database is being accessed.

---

[2]https://www.phptherightway.com/#databases

Assetic

A real-world example of a package that contains classes that are closed against many different kinds of changes is the `kriswallsmith/assetic` package,[3] which contains the Assetic library[4] used for managing web assets (e.g., combining, compressing, and filtering JS and CSS files).

Looking at its directory structure (see Listing 8-1; I've removed many files to make the picture clearer), you can see that it contains the core classes as well as many classes called "filters," which are used to modify the contents of an asset file (e.g., to compile Less to CSS, compress JS, etc.).

Listing 8-1. The Directory Tree of the kriswallsmith/assetic Package (Abbreviated)

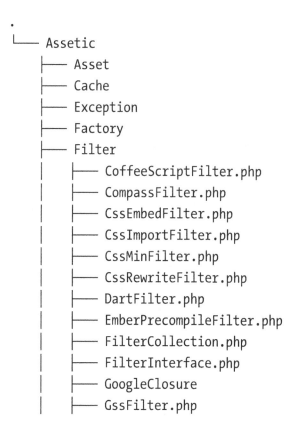

```
.
└── Assetic
    ├── Asset
    ├── Cache
    ├── Exception
    ├── Factory
    ├── Filter
    │   ├── CoffeeScriptFilter.php
    │   ├── CompassFilter.php
    │   ├── CssEmbedFilter.php
    │   ├── CssImportFilter.php
    │   ├── CssMinFilter.php
    │   ├── CssRewriteFilter.php
    │   ├── DartFilter.php
    │   ├── EmberPrecompileFilter.php
    │   ├── FilterCollection.php
    │   ├── FilterInterface.php
    │   ├── GoogleClosure
    │   ├── GssFilter.php
```

[3]https://packagist.org/packages/kriswallsmith/assetic
[4]https://github.com/kriswallsmith/assetic

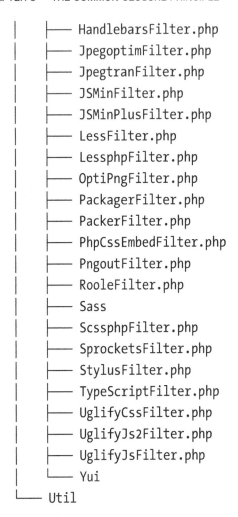

```
|       ├──── HandlebarsFilter.php
|       ├──── JpegoptimFilter.php
|       ├──── JpegtranFilter.php
|       ├──── JSMinFilter.php
|       ├──── JSMinPlusFilter.php
|       ├──── LessFilter.php
|       ├──── LessphpFilter.php
|       ├──── OptiPngFilter.php
|       ├──── PackagerFilter.php
|       ├──── PackerFilter.php
|       ├──── PhpCssEmbedFilter.php
|       ├──── PngoutFilter.php
|       ├──── RooleFilter.php
|       ├──── Sass
|       ├──── ScssphpFilter.php
|       ├──── SprocketsFilter.php
|       ├──── StylusFilter.php
|       ├──── TypeScriptFilter.php
|       ├──── UglifyCssFilter.php
|       ├──── UglifyJs2Filter.php
|       ├──── UglifyJsFilter.php
|       └──── Yui
└──── Util
```

At first glance, this package clearly violates the *Common Reuse* principle. It's obvious that not all classes in this package will be used together, since many of the filters aren't used at the same time by the same user. Maybe each user really requires just two or three of them.

But when we switch our perspective from the user to the package maintainer and try to apply the *Common Closure* principle, we should notice that these classes are *not all closed* against the same kinds of changes. For example, if anything changes with regard to the way the Less compiler works, or the type of input that the RooleFilter expects, a change will be made in just one or two classes inside the package. Afterwards the package maintainer needs to release a new version of the *entire package* to make the changes available to all its users. This will require people to upgrade their projects (and probably also bring in many unrelated changes from the repository), which may or may not have unwanted side-effects.

To make Assetic comply with the *Common Closure* principle its maintainer should create separate packages for each filter. Each filter-specific package will only be sensitive to specific kinds of changes (namely changes related to its own dependencies, like the Less compiler). The main `assetic` package will not be affected by any such change. When one of the specialized filters changes, only a new version of the filter-specific package needs to be released. In such cases, there will be no need to release a new version of the main `assetic` package.

Adhering to the *Common Closure* principle with regard to changes made in (optional) dependencies will thus prevent unnecessary package releases. This will effectively lower the burden on your users. They don't need to upgrade their dependencies because of changes that don't apply to them.

A Change in an Application Layer

The first kind of change we discussed was somewhat external to the package: it was caused by a change in one of its dependencies, be it a package, an extension, or the programming language itself. The second kind of change is related to something called *architectural layers*.

Layers are a way to apply the *Single Responsibility* principle to an application. One traditional method of layering an application is by separating the model from the view and putting controllers in between. The controllers will regulate traffic from the front controller down into the model and back to the view. Depending on who you to talk to, other divisions may make more sense. Personally I like to use separate *Domain, Application,* and *Infrastructure* layers in my applications (if you want to know the details, take a look at my article "Layers, Ports, & Adapters - Part 2, Layers"[5]). No matter what kind of rules you apply, layering is always a useful organizational pattern for applications.

Most applications already apply some grouping along the lines of the application's subdomains, or sets of related features. The resulting groups are often called *modules*. Defining modules should be considered *vertical* slicing, since the code for each of the modules will be more or less independent of other modules.

Each of the modules can also be *horizontally* sliced by designating parts of those modules to their own *layers*. It's useful to have a set of conventions for these layers. This helps developers find the right place for every file. Combined with rules about how these

---

[5]`https://matthiasnoback.nl/2017/08/layers-ports-and-adapters-part-2-layers/`

layers can use each other's code, you can make the design of each module very flexible. For instance, pushing all the presentation logic into the *Infrastructure* layer, you would make it possible to rewrite this logic using a different templating engine, or switch from HTML pages to JSON responses, without the need to change any of the code in the other layers (i.e., *Application* and *Domain*).

Although application modules usually shouldn't end up in packages (we'll talk about this at the end of the chapter), you may still want to reuse (part of) a module. You may be tempted to take out those files that you want to reuse and put them all in one package. This will make code for all the application layers end up in a single package.

Now remember that you introduced the layering to allow swapping out (part of) one layer, without requiring a change to any of the other layers. Considering the *Common Closure* principle again, we wouldn't want changes to be made to only one layer within a package, and not to the others. If that's bound to happen, the principle encourages us to split the package, and in this case it means we have to split it according to its layers.

Each package will then have code for only one layer, and will therefore be closed against the same kinds of changes. It would also allow users to depend on the *Domain* and *Application* packages of the reusable module, but implement all the infrastructure code themselves.

FOSUserBundle

Let's take a look at a real-world example of a package that uses layers—the `friendsofsymfony/user-bundle`[6] package, which contains the `FOSUserBundle`.[7] It can be used in a Symfony application as a way to quickly set up user management. Out-of-the-box it provides several useful things that almost every web application needs:

- Persistent users and user groups

- A password reset page

- A registration page

- A change password page

- User management from the command-line

- ...

---

[6]https://packagist.org/packages/friendsofsymfony/user-bundle
[7]https://github.com/FriendsOfSymfony/FOSUserBundle/

Looking at the directory structure (see Listing 8-2), you can roughly recognize these features in the files that are present.

Listing 8-2. The Directory Tree of the friendsofsymfony/user-bundle Package (Abbreviated)

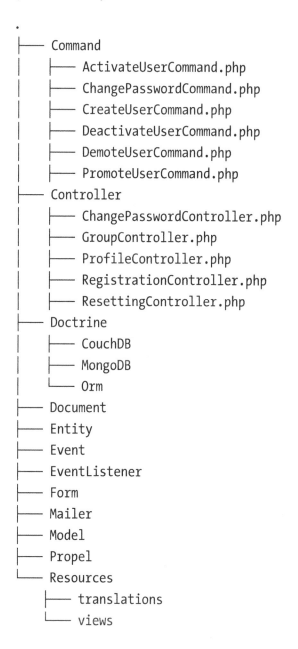

```
.
├── Command
│   ├── ActivateUserCommand.php
│   ├── ChangePasswordCommand.php
│   ├── CreateUserCommand.php
│   ├── DeactivateUserCommand.php
│   ├── DemoteUserCommand.php
│   └── PromoteUserCommand.php
├── Controller
│   ├── ChangePasswordController.php
│   ├── GroupController.php
│   ├── ProfileController.php
│   ├── RegistrationController.php
│   └── ResettingController.php
├── Doctrine
│   ├── CouchDB
│   ├── MongoDB
│   └── Orm
├── Document
├── Entity
├── Event
├── EventListener
├── Form
├── Mailer
├── Model
├── Propel
└── Resources
    ├── translations
    └── views
```

Coincidentally, this is another example of a package that violates the *Common Reuse* principle because it's quite possible that someone would want to use only the model classes that are provided by this package in their own project, which is not a Symfony application. There's no way to do it without pulling in the entire user-bundle package, which is otherwise quite useless to them.

The same objection to the particular lack of cohesion of this package arises when we consider the *Common Closure* principle with regard to application layers. It's immediately clear that this package contains code related to all kinds of layers. Therefore a change in requirements related to the user model would result in just a few modifications within this package. Many files will remain untouched. The same goes for a visual makeover of the web pages provided by this package. To make the new templates available to everyone, a new release needs to be issued, which is irrelevant to everyone who uses their own templates. Because some other things may have changed in the new release, users would still need to verify that their application is not broken after upgrading their dependencies.

Following the *Common Closure* principle with respect to application layers would therefore require the package maintainer to split this package according to the different layers for which it contains code and other resources. That way only relevant changes will cause users to upgrade their dependencies. At the same time, it allows users to replace one layer implementation provided by the package maintainer with their own implementation, without the need to pull unused code into their projects.

THE PROBLEM WITH PLUGINS FOR FRAMEWORKS

Most frameworks for web applications offer an all-round solution for each of the traditional application layers (model, view, and controller). Although this idea is quite outdated and many people have been experimenting with other types of layers and architectures, still some applications can be reduced to these main layers. You always need some model of the domain of your business. You always need a way to show something to a user of your application, and you always need something that the framework can invoke in order to put things in motion.

Whenever a new framework starts to attract attention from developers, everything that already exists will be recreated to work well with that particular framework. And since the framework provides a standard way of doing things in each layer, you will end up with packages…

- For Symfony, called "bundles," that use Twig for views and Doctrine ORM for persistence

- For Laravel, called "packages," that use Blade for views and Eloquent ORM for persistence

- For Zend Framework, called "modules," that use Zend_View for views and Zend_Db for persistence

- …

This doesn't make sense. It means that reuse is actually obstructed, because of the *narrowness of the area of reuse*. If the maintainers of these packages would care more about package design principles, they would split their packages according to responsibilities, with respect to dependencies as well as application layers and subject matter. This way, there would only need to be one package that modeled the domain. There would be several packages that implemented persistence for domain objects using different kinds of database and persistence libraries. And there would also be several packages that provided a presentation layer that works with different templating engines. Separating packages like this would make true reuse possible (at least between projects that use the same programming language).

A Change in the Business

We have considered layers as a way to partition your packages. Each package should contain code that's related to only one application layer. That way, when a requirement changes with regard to other layers, the package will remain untouched.

When you follow the *Common Closure* principle with regard to layers, you end up with packages that all have just one of the big responsibilities (like modeling things, presenting things, etc.). Nevertheless, these packages would still contain code that's likely to be modified for entirely different reasons. A package that contains all the code of the domain layer, would contain classes that model a person, an article, an address, a payment, etc. Whenever the requirements of the domain layer change because of business reasons ("we need to support another payment type"), only one file in the domain package will be modified, and the other ones will stay as they were before the requirements changed.

This of course looks like another violation of the *Common Closure* principle since the classes in a package should be closed against the same kinds of changes. A package entirely dedicated to the domain layer is closed against all different kinds of changes. When you need to decide how to group classes into packages, you therefore need to consider business changes as one kind of change to close classes against.

Sylius

Let me end this section with a *good* example of a project that separates packages by domain. It's the Sylius project[8] and it offers one big `sylius/sylius` package[9] containing multiple smaller packages (using Git subtree splits), nicely divided by subject matter (see Listing 8-3).

Listing 8-3. Sub-Packages of the sylius/sylius Package

```
SyliusAddressingBundle
SyliusCartBundle
SyliusFlowBundle
SyliusInventoryBundle
SyliusOmnipayBundle
SyliusOrderBundle
SyliusProductBundle
SyliusPromotionsBundle
SyliusResourceBundle
SyliusSettingsBundle
SyliusShippingBundle
SyliusTaxationBundle
SyliusTaxonomiesBundle
SyliusVariableProductBundle
```

Although none of these packages has been split according to architectural layers, when it comes to the problem domain, these packages are all nicely separated from each other. This way the maintainer will be able to limit modifications necessitated by changing requirements to just one or two packages at a time.

---

[8]https://sylius.com/
[9]https://packagist.org/packages/sylius/sylius

Packaging Business Logic

In this chapter, we've covered various topics from the realm of application development (as opposed to *package* development). We talked about architectural layering—something that's usually considered within the context of an application, not a package. We also talked about domain or business logic and why you should limit a package to a particular subdomain. Again, this separation into subdomains is usually considered within a larger software project only, not as often in the context of package development.

The reason is that using architectural layers and dividing a domain into subdomains is usually only needed when there's a fair amount of code. Since the three cohesion principles will lead to smaller packages in general, there isn't a lot of code left to layer or divide. You'll find that most packages therefore belong to just one layer, and don't even span multiple subdomains. Let's take a look at the bigger picture, to find out why this happens.

Every application needs a user management system, a login page, a password reset page, some way to keep track of user rights, some management modules where administrators can quickly go into the database and change something for the customer, etc. As a programmer, you may sometimes feel like you're only getting to the heart of the matter after weeks of laying out technical foundations like these for a new application. This means that intuitively you know which part of the overall business domain is central to the application you're working on now, and which ones are much less relevant.

Of course, a login system should be in place. It should function correctly and be secure. But a login system is something that many more teams need and it doesn't have to be reinvented again and again. Instead, it would be smart to get done with this part of your application as soon as possible, and start working on the parts where your application can really make a difference.

Eric Evans summarizes his advice on this topic as follows:

> *Identify cohesive subdomains that are not the motivation for your project. Factor out generic models of these subdomains and place them in separate modules. Leave no trace of your specialties in them. Once they have been separated, give their continuing development lower priority than the core domain, and avoid assigning your core developers to the tasks (because they will gain little domain knowledge from them). Also consider off-the-shelf solutions or published models for these generic subdomains.*[10]

---

[10]Eric Evans, *Domain-Driven Design*, Addison-Wesley Professional (2003)

He calls this *strategic distillation*—finding out what your core domain is, thereby recognizing subdomains, including "generic" ones. For *application* developers, this is useful advice, because it helps you focus your development effort on areas where your application can stand out among many others. At the same time, it will help you decide for which parts of your application you should rather use an existing library or external service, also known as an "off-the-shelf solution".

For *package* developers, this is useful advice too, because application developers looking for off-the-shelf solutions can be the *users* of the packages you publish. So when you consider extracting part of your application into a reusable package, consider if it can be used by others to help them get to their core domain quicker. The `FOSUserBundle` is an excellent example of such a package that looks like it has been extracted from a project in order to be reused again and again in every project that needs user management and a login system.

You can also create a larger reusable package or a set of packages and include with it a full-fledged domain model and application services (like Sylius does for e-commerce software). It will be a challenge to make packages like these useful for all users, because the code in it is bound to be specific to some understanding of the business domain. This means that users will want to change baked-in behavior. As soon as this happens, however, users will also have to evaluate whether they have properly separated their core and generic subdomains. Reusable code is mostly successful for generic subdomains; a core domain needs a custom modeling effort to get it *just right*. And to make it easier to evolve with changing business requirements.

Because the classes you write for subdomains other than the generic ones are likely to be very specific and not useful in other projects. don't put them in packages. Just use namespaces to group classes into the subdomains they belong to. Likewise, you can use namespaces to structure application code according to the architectural layers you want to apply. This will save you a lot of frustration when you're working on the application. A change to the application can be released in one go, even if it spans multiple layers and subdomains. If instead you create packages for every combination of architectural layer and subdomain, you will soon end up with an unmaintainable application that's very resistant to change.

The Tension Triangle of Cohesion Principles

Before we continue with the next set of package design principles related to coupling, we will briefly discuss an interesting concept mentioned by Robert Martin in one of his training videos on cleancoders.com.[11] It's called the *tension triangle of cohesion principles,* as shown in Figure 8-1.

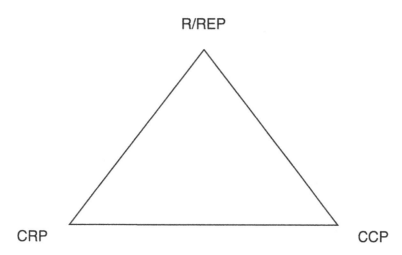

Figure 8-1. *Tension triangle of cohesion principles*

You can draw a triangle within each corner one of the package cohesion principles. Then you can locate any package somewhere within that triangle. Moving a package to one of the corners means that it implements that principle maximally, while it neglects the other principles. Moving to the vertex opposite to one of the corners means that the package definitely does not follow the corresponding principle, but follows the other principles equally well.

What Robert suggests is that a package may move within the diagram. When you first start working on a project, packages may be primarily designed according to the *Common Reuse* principle. Later on you may choose to follow the *Common Closure* principle more strictly because that will ease maintenance. Then in the end, you may focus on making the package reusable so that all the effort you put into it will give you an advantage in your next project (or will help other developers around the world solve the problems you have already solved quite well).

---

[11]https://cleancoders.com/episode/clean-code-episode-16/show

The tension triangle is a nice way to estimate the quality of the cohesion of a package at any moment in time. It's easy to notice when a package doesn't follow the *Release/Reuse Equivalence* principle, because then it's hard to add it as a dependency to your project and difficult to keep it up-to-date once you've managed to do so. It's also easy to verify how well the *Common Reuse* principle is obeyed—when you feel like you have to pull in a lot of code, just to use one or two classes, then something is wrong. And finally if the package contains classes that have responsibilities in many different fields of expertise, the *Common Closure* principle is not followed very well. Drawing a triangle for one of your packages might help you find out how to improve it.

Conclusion

When some aspect of a package needs to change, it has to be "opened". The code has to be modified, and the updated package needs to be released again. It will be easier for the maintainer of the package if it doesn't have to be modified and released again for all kinds of reasons. Therefore, the *Common Closure* principle tells us to consider all the reasons a package might need to change, and to split it accordingly. This will eventually make each package "closed against the same kinds of changes".

Common reasons for opening a package are:

- If something changes about a dependency (e.g., it needs to be upgraded, or it needs to be replaced).

- If requirements have changed regarding a piece of business logic.

- If part of the infrastructure changes, but the core logic remains as it is (e.g., when you change the layout of the UI, or if you switch to a different database).

When you're a package maintainer, keep track of how many packages need to be released again after a change. Aim to minimize this number by splitting the package. Also keep track of how many classes are modified for every release. If this is only a fraction of all the classes in that package, split the package. Moving out the classes that rarely change, or change for different reasons, will ease future maintenance. It will be good for the users too, since they won't need to upgrade the package for reasons that are not relevant to them.

CHAPTER 9

The Acyclic Dependencies Principle

As I explained in the introduction to the package design principles, all programmers develop a sense of "belonging together". But next to this intuition with regard to cohesion, programmers also have a nose for coupling. Looking at a piece of code, they will be able to figure out what it is coupled to. As their careers progress, they will develop an ever stronger "coupling radar" by figuring out the actual *dependencies* of any piece of code.

Coupling: Discovering Dependencies

Looking at some code, you can ask yourself, on which other *things* does this code rely in order to be successfully executed? Thinking long and hard about this question reveals some obvious dependencies, but probably also some less obvious, or indirect, dependencies.

Consider the Kernel class defined in Listing 9-1.

Listing 9-1. The Kernel Class

```
namespace SomeFramework;

class Kernel
{
    public function __construct(EventDispatcher $eventDispatcher)
    {
        // ...
    }
}
```

© Matthias Noback 2018
M. Noback, *Principles of Package Design*, https://doi.org/10.1007/978-1-4842-4119-6_9

In order to be used successfully in an application, the `Kernel` class depends on:

- The `EventDispatcher` class. It gets an instance of this class injected as a constructor argument.

- The PHP interpreter. It needs this in order to be run at all. More specifically, the version of the PHP interpreter should be at least 5.3, since the class resides in a namespace that's not supported by earlier PHP versions.

We could go much, much further in specifying dependencies. A PHP interpreter depends on an operating system, running on a computer, which needs power and should be accessible to you as the user of this software. It should therefore be in this world, this universe (well, maybe your code is even cross-universe compatible, who knows?), and so on.

I agree with you, that this is taking things too far. However, merely looking at the classes used in the code and the PHP version that is required to run the code is not sufficient in most cases. Some code may rely on a database server being up and running and reachable from the server on which the code is being executed. Or maybe a certain amount of memory is required to run the code, or the user who runs the software should have certain filesystem rights, etc.

In this chapter and in the next two chapters, we discuss package dependencies. When we discuss the coupling principles for packages, we won't consider the physical dependencies of a package. We only take other units of code—external to the package—into consideration. These *external units of code* can be actual packages (with or without a package definition file), language extensions (which are really a special kind of packages themselves), or other conglomerates of code that are necessary to run the code in a given package.

Different Ways of Package Coupling

Let's first settle on the following convention: we call "the given package" the "root package". Starting with any root package, we can enumerate the dependencies of that package. Those dependencies can be any kind of package, or even a language extension, but we just call those dependencies "packages" too, for simplicity's sake.

Now we can make a list of ways in which the code in the root package introduces dependencies on other packages. As a package maintainer we need this list when we are collecting the names of required packages for our package definition file. We also need this list of dependencies when we are going to apply the package coupling principles. When we don't know exactly in which ways the code in the root package introduces coupling to other packages, we won't know how to draw a dependency graph of the root package as part of a larger system of packages. We also won't know how to fix problems in the dependency graph.

Composition

We already looked at one particular way of coupling: when the type of a constructor argument is a class (see Listing 9-2).

Listing 9-2. Coupling Through Constructor Arguments

```
namespace RootPackage;

use OtherPackage\EventDispatcher;

class Kernel
{
    private $eventDispatcher;

    public function __construct(EventDispatcher $eventDispatcher)
    {
        $this->eventDispatcher = $eventDispatcher;
    }
}
```

The Kernel class is in the root package. When the EventDispatcher class is in another package (as it should be), this particular piece of code introduces package coupling. For example, the kernel package would depend on the event-dispatcher package. This is called a dependency *by composition*, because the pattern of storing one object inside another object for later use is called "composition".

Inheritance

Another way in which a class can be coupled to another class is by inheriting from it (see Listing 9-3).

Listing 9-3. Coupling Through Inheritance

```
namespace RootPackage;

use OtherPackage\Controller;

class LoginController extends Controller
{
    // ...
}
```

When the parent class `Controller` (or any of its parent classes) is in another package than the `LoginController`, inheritance introduces package coupling.

Implementation

Very much like inheritance, implementing an interface or extending an abstract class and implementing its abstract methods introduces coupling too (see Listing 9-4).

Listing 9-4. Coupling Through Implementing an Interface

```
namespace RootPackage;

use OtherPackage\RequestListener;

class IpBlocker implements RequestListener
{
    // ...
}
```

Usage

Often coupling between classes occurs when an instance of one class simply *uses* an instance of another class, for instance, as one of its method parameters (see Listing 9-5).

Listing 9-5. Coupling Through Method Arguments

```
namespace RootPackage;

use OtherPackage\NewRequestEvent;

class IpBlocker
{
    public function onKernelRequest(NewRequestEvent $event): void
    {
        // ...
    }
}
```

Object Instantiation

In the previous examples, dependencies on classes outside the root package were out in the open, because they were part of the public interface (a parent class, an implemented interface, and a type of a method argument). But there are also some more private ways of coupling. For instance, when one object creates other objects of a class inside another package (see Listing 9-6).

Listing 9-6. Coupling Through Object Instantiation

```
namespace RootPackage;

use OtherPackage\ServiceContainer;

class Kernel
{
    public function boot(): void
    {
        $container = new ServiceContainer();

        // ...
    }
}
```

Global Function Usage

The usual suspects for coupling are classes, but you shouldn't forget to look at the functions that are used in a package. Many functions are only available when a particular package or language extension has been installed, for instance, the curl PHP extension (see Listing 9-7).

Listing 9-7. Coupling Through Function Usage

```
class HttpClient
{
    public function send(): void
    {
        $ch = curl_init();

        // ...
    }
}
```

Functions are only used in the internal parts of a class, i.e. inside the body of its methods. So spotting these dependencies takes a bit more effort. The same goes for public static methods, which also introduce coupling inside methods, as shown in Listing 9-8.

Listing 9-8. Coupling Through Public Static Method Usage

```
class Controller
{
    public function indexAction()
    {
        $translator = Zend_Registry::get('Zend_Translator');

        // ...
    }
}
```

Not to Be Considered: Global State

Code in a package often relies on a particular global state. The most obvious example is that each package implicitly relies on the presence of an autoloader, which is able to (auto)load the classes inside the package.

Depending on global state should otherwise always be avoided, but even when it happens, we don't consider it a package dependency in this book, since we can't make it explicit inside the list of requirements of a package.

Visualizing Dependencies

Before we can start to apply the coupling principles to our package design, we need to be able to visualize any current state of package coupling. When we do this, we only consider one system (i.e., application) at a time. We take all the packages inside that system and, one by one, consider them as a root package. We then use this list of coupling types (e.g. composition, inheritance, etc.) to extract a list of all the dependencies of classes in this package. As soon as such a class dependency goes beyond the boundaries of the package itself, it should be marked as a *package dependency*.

The result of such an exercise is a list like this:

- Package A depends on Package C

- Package B depends on Packages A and D

- Package C depends on Package B

Packages and their dependencies, when written down as shown in Figure 9-1, form a recipe for a graph, where each package is a *vertex* (node) and each dependency is an *edge* (line).

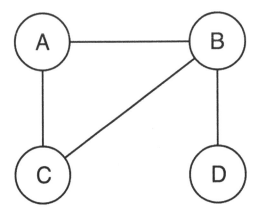

Figure 9-1. *A graph with vertices as packages and edges as dependencies*

Since dependencies have directionality (a package depends on another package, not automatically the other way around), we can convert the graph into a directed graph by simply adding some arrows to the lines, as shown in Figure 9-2.

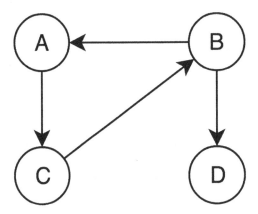

Figure 9-2. *A directed graph*

What's left out of these diagrams are self-referencing packages. These aren't of interest at this point, although I will briefly get back to this subject later. Almost all packages are self-referencing actually, because often a class in a root package uses another class or a function from the same package.

When it comes to package dependencies, there is another important aspect that we need to take into consideration when we draw the dependency graph of packages within a system: there are probably some version constraints with regard to the dependencies.

For instance, Package C may require at least version 1.0 of Package B. We can write these constraints as annotations in the graph, as shown in Figure 9-3.

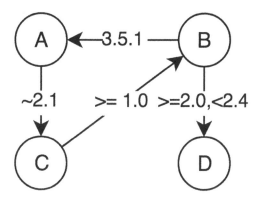

Figure 9-3. *A directed graph with annotations for version constraints*

The Acyclic Dependencies Principle

With all this acquired knowledge about package coupling, it's only one small step toward the explanation of the *Acyclic Dependencies* principle. The principle states that:

> *The dependency structure between packages must be a directed acyclic graph; that is, there must be no cycles in the dependency structure.*[1]

We already discussed how you can figure out the actual dependencies of all the packages in a system, then draw a *directed graph* of the outcome. The only missing piece of information is what an *acyclic* directed graph is.

A directed graph has no cycles if, starting from any vertex, there is no path that via any number of vertices leads back to the original vertex. Such a directed graph is called an *acyclic* graph. Translated to the language of dependency graphs—whichever package you take as the root package, by following the dependency arrows, you will not be able to return to the root package. See Figure 9-4.

---

[1]Robert C. Martin, Engineering Notebook, C++ Report, Nov-Dec, 1996 (PDF available on `http://butunclebob.com/ArticleS.UncleBob.PrinciplesOfOod`).

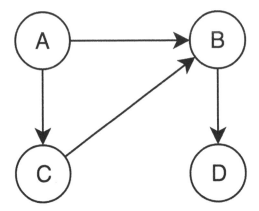

Figure 9-4. *An acyclic directed graph: no cycles*

Conversely, if a directed graph *has* cycles, it means that there is *at least one* vertex for which you can find a path that leads back to that same vertex. In terms of a dependency graph, this means that there is at least one package that is the beginning of a path of subsequent dependencies that leads back to that same package (see Figure 9-5).

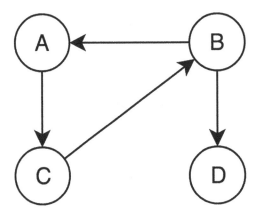

Figure 9-5. *A cyclic directed graph: one cycle*

The *Acyclic Dependencies* principle just says that when you draw your dependency graph, it should look like an *acyclic directed graph*, meaning that it has no cycles.

Problematic Cycles

As a programmer you're likely familiar with cycles, often caused by mistakes easily made, like the one shown in (see Listing 9-9).

Listing 9-9. Programming Mistakes with Cycles

```php
$somethingThatIsAlwaysTrue = ...;

while ($somethingThatIsAlwaysTrue) {
    // ...
}

// or something similar:
for ($i = 0; $i < 100;) {
    // we forgot to increment...
}

// but also:
class Node
{
    private $parent;

    public function getParent(): ?Node
    {
        if ($this->parent) {
            return $this->parent;
        }

        // hmm
        return $this->getParent();
    }
}
```

An example of a common type of cycle that's not really a mistake, but more a design issue, is shown in Listing 9-10.

Listing 9-10. Desk and Programmer Need an Instance of Each Other

```php
class Desk
{
    private $programmer;

    public function __construct(Programmer $programmer)
    {
        $this->programmer = $programmer;
```

```php
    }
}

class Programmer
{
    private $desk;

    public function __construct(Desk $desk)
    {
        $this->desk = $desk;
    }
}

$desk = new Desk($programmer);
$programmer = new Programmer($desk);
// ??
```

No matter how hard we try, we won't get this straight. It's a real circular dependency. We first need to instantiate a Desk, but in order to do that we need a Programmer, who needs a Desk, etc.

We commonly fix issues like these by first constructing an object, then injecting the dependency that caused the cycle (see Listing 9-11).

Listing 9-11. Breaking the Cycle

```php
class Desk
{
    private $programmer;

    public function setProgrammer(Programmer $programmer): void
    {
        $this->programmer = $programmer;
    }
}

class Programmer
{
    private $desk;

    public function __construct(Desk $desk)
```

```
    {
        $desk->setProgrammer($this);

        $this->desk = $desk;
    }
}

$desk = new Desk();
$programmer = new Programmer($desk);
```

When you use this solution, you can be sure that at one point in time *at least one* of the objects is in an invalid state. In this case it's the Desk object. It has no associated Programmer until it has been assigned in the constructor of the Programmer itself, so this isn't the ultimate solution.

Instead of sacrificing consistent state for our objects, we should find a way to break the cycle. In real-world modeling situations you may ask the following questions to find a better solution:

- Is it really the entire object you need, or just part of it, maybe even a single value? If you only need part of the object, you can inject that part, and effectively remove the cycle.

- Do these two objects really need to know about each other? Is it possible to change the relationship from a bidirectional to a unidirectional one?

Cycles in a Package Dependency Graph

The problems described previously usually don't travel across package boundaries, but remain private to the package and should be fixed there. However, when a circular dependency between classes goes beyond the boundary of their containing package, it does become a *circular dependency between packages* and then some other, bigger problems arise.

For some package or dependency managers it may be impossible to resolve circular dependencies. This is the same for dependency injection, a.k.a. service containers, which may not be able to instantiate services if their dependencies form a cycle too (e.g., if service B depends on service A, but eventually it turns out that A's instantiation depends on the proper instantiation of service B).

But even if the resolution of circular dependencies is not a problem for your package manager of choice, release management of circular dependencies can still be problematic. Imagine how releasing the next major version of Package A will be depending on the next major version of Package B, which is being rewritten to take full advantage of all the good things to be released with the next major version of Package A. Which package should be released first?

It *will* be difficult to coordinate major releases when a dependency graph has cycles, although this can be overcome by doing "kamikaze" releases, adding some backward or forward compatibility measures, and providing friendly version constraints for the package dependencies involved. In the end this may not cause you too much pain. The problem of circular package dependencies is actually much bigger with programming languages that have a build process. When dependencies of the build process are being resolved, a circular dependency may even prevent the entire build process from succeeding.

Still, there's the programmer's intuition that something is wrong about cycles in software, in particular cycles that transcend the boundaries of one package. So you may want to fix them anyway. The good news is that there are some easy solutions to remove cycles from a dependency graph.

Solutions for Breaking the Cycles

In the first place, some cycles are "more real" than other cycles.

Some Pseudo-Cycles and Their Dissolution

Consider the two packages shown in Figure 9-6, which have a direct dependency on each other (it doesn't really matter for this example whether or not the cycle consists of more packages).

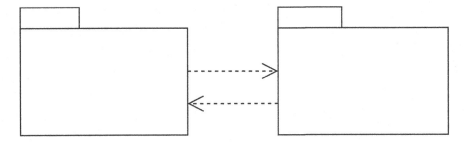

Figure 9-6. *Two packages that are dependent on each other*

When a dependency is considered a "package dependency," this means that part of the code in the *root* package depends on a part of the code in the *other* package. Most often the root package contains a class that uses a class from the other package in one of the ways described at the beginning of this chapter. When zooming in on both packages, we discover in this case that, indeed, one class in the root package (Class A) depends on a class in the other package (Class C), which explains one direction of the package dependency (see Figure 9-7).

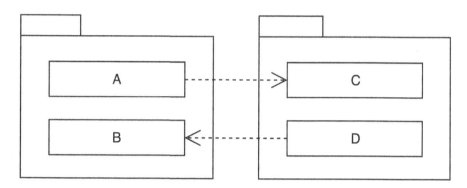

Figure 9-7. *Zooming in on the actual dependencies*

Trying to explain the reason why this package dependency is *circular*, we notice that the reciprocal dependency is totally unnecessary, because it concerns two other, unrelated classes—Classes B and D.

This means that these two packages are used in two different, unrelated ways and that the classes have not been divided correctly among the two. These packages simply violate the *Common Reuse* principle: not all of their classes are reused together at the same time. This is also reminiscent of the *Interface Segregation* principle (Chapter 4), but applied to the package itself instead of just one class. Apparently there are multiple different *clients* for this package, and only some of them cause a dependency cycle.

I call this type of dependency cycle a *pseudo-cycle*. It can easily be dissolved by rearranging the code and creating one or two new packages. For instance, you can put Classes B and D together in one package, which makes the dependency internal to that package, as shown in Figure 9-8.

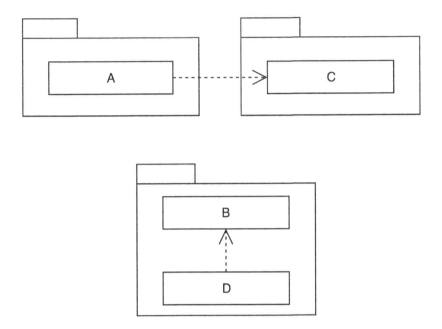

Figure 9-8. *One solution for dissolving the pseudo-cycle*

Or you can put Classes B and D in their own separate packages, which leaves the package dependency as it is, but at least removes the cycle from the dependency graph (see Figure 9-9).

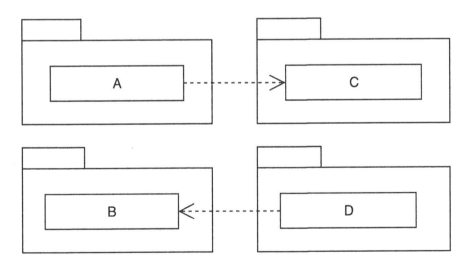

Figure 9-9. *Another solution for dissolving the pseudo-cycle*

You should choose the second solution when other parts of the system rely on just Class B or just Class D, which would mean that according to the *Common Reuse* principle, these classes should be in separate packages.

Some Real Cycles and Their Dissolution

We've discussed a nice pseudo-cycle, but what does a real cycle look like? Figure 9-10 shows a schematic example of such a circular dependency relation.

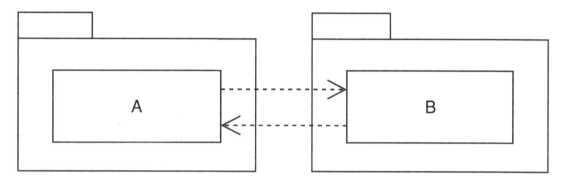

Figure 9-10. *A real cycle*

Again, there may be any number of packages between these two, as long as there is an actual cycle.

To make this a bit more concrete, let's say Class A is used to process web forms and Class B is a generic validator. Forms and validation are very much related, but at least validation is not limited to forms. So the validation package should be available for separate use in different scenarios (for instance, to validate query parameters or deserialized objects).

In the form package, we find the Form class (see Listing 9-12).

Listing 9-12. The Form Class from the Form Package

```
use Validator\Validator;

class Form
{
    private $validator;
    private $errors = [];
```

```php
    public function __construct(Validator $validator)
    {
        $this->validator = $validator;
    }

    public function isValid(): bool
    {
        $this->validator->validateForm($this);

        return count($this->errors) === 0;
    }

    public function addError(Error $error): void
    {
        $this->errors[] = $error;
    }
}
```

In the validator package, we find the Validator class (see Listing 9-13).

Listing 9-13. The Validator Class from the Validator Package

```php
use Form\Form;

class Validator
{
    public function validateForm(Form $form): void
    {
        // ...

        $form->addError(...);
    }
}
```

These code snippets expose a circular dependency between Validator and Form of type "usage" (see the list of coupling types at the beginning of this chapter).

To break this type of cycle, it won't suffice to merely move code around (like it did when we discussed a pseudo-cycle in the previous section). We must do some actual programming to fix this problem. We will refactor the code, i.e. change its structure, not its behavior, by applying some design patterns to it. There are many conceivable solutions and I will show some of the most used ones.

Dependency Inversion

The first thing we can do is remove the hard dependency on a class in another package. As explained in Chapter 5, by applying the *Dependency Inversion* principle, we can easily revert dependency directions by depending on something *abstract*, i.e. an interface, instead of something *concrete*, i.e. a class. If we then move the interfaces to separate packages, we are saved (see Listing 9-14).

Listing 9-14. Introducing a FormInterface and a ValidatorInterface

```
interface FormInterface
{
    public function isValid(): bool;

    public function addError(Error $error): void;
}

class Form implements FormInterface
{
    public function __construct(ValidatorInterface $validator)
    {
        // ...
    }

    public function isValid(): bool
    {
        // ...
    }

    public function addError(Error $error)
    {
        // ...
    }
}

interface ValidatorInterface
{
    public function validateForm(FormInterface $form): void;
}
```

203

```
class Validator implements ValidatorInterface
{
    public function validateForm(FormInterface $form): void
    {
        // ...
    }
}
```

We introduce interfaces and we make the existing classes implement those interfaces. Then we use only the interfaces as parameter types, not the classes. When we put the interfaces in separate packages, we have successfully diverted some of the problematic dependencies and there are strictly no circles left in the dependency graph, as shown in Figure 9-11.

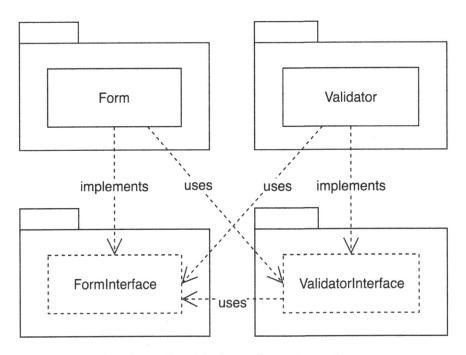

Figure 9-11. *Removing the cycle with dependency inversion*

The real trick here is that even though Form originally depended on an instance of Validator (injected as a constructor argument), FormInterface doesn't, which means there is no dependency arrow from FormInterface to ValidatorInterface.

So, using dependency inversion, we have actually dissolved the cycle in the dependency graph. However, it's not really the best solution there is, since we also had to move Form to its own package.

Inversion of Control

The design problem with the Form and Validator classes that caused them to be tightly coupled is that they know too much about each other, and this results in lots of communication back and forth between them. Remember, the reason for having a separate package for data validation was that data validation is not necessarily limited to validation of data submitted using a web form. So it is surprising to say the least that the Validator class actually has a validateForm() method. This clearly violates the *Interface Segregation* principle (Chapter 4), since only a portion of the *clients* of the Validator class will use that method.

When an object communicates with another object by calling methods on it, it really exercises control over it. Calling a method triggers an action in the other object. When objects call each other's methods, i.e. *communicate with each other*, this should thus be seen as *exercising control* over each other. But communication that goes back and forth creates a cycle. To resolve that cycle, we must break the communication lines between objects and let some intermediate object do the talking. This would basically *invert* the direction of the controlling behavior of these objects. Hence this technique is known as *inversion of control*.

There are quite a lot of options when you want to refactor code that is too much "in control". In fact, all the design patterns known as "behavioral patterns" (see also the famous "Gang of Four" book entitled *Design Patterns: Elements of Reusable Object-Oriented Software*) are suitable for this purpose. It's still up to you to judge if they apply to your situation. Also, you don't necessarily need to follow the exact patterns.

Mediator

The first and easiest solution is to use the *Mediator* pattern.[2] The Form object then shouldn't make any direct calls to a Validator object anymore. Instead, it may only call the mediator, which on its turn will make any form-specific calls to the Validator (see Listing 9-15).

---

[2]Erich Gamma e.a., *Design Patterns: Elements of Reusable Object-Oriented Software,* Addison-Wesley, 1994.

Listing 9-15. The FormValidationMediator

```
class FormValidationMediator
{
    private $validator;

    public function __construct(ValidatorInterface $validator)
    {
        $this->validator = $validator;
    }

    public function validate(FormInterface $form): void
    {
        $formData = $form->getData();

        $errors = $this->validator->validate($formData);

        foreach ($errors as $error) {
            $form->addError($error);
        }
    }
}

class Form implements FormInterface
{
    private $formValidator;

    public function __construct(
        FormValidationMediator $formValidator
    ) {
        $this->formValidator = $formValidator;
    }

    public function isValid(): bool
    {
        // the FormValidationMediator will add errors to the form
        $this->formValidator->validate($this);

        return count($this->errors) === 0;
    }
}
```

This basically removes the dependency from the validator package to the form package. Validator is now truly standalone. The mediator that runs validation on forms should be in its own package, having dependencies on both the form and the validator interface packages, as shown in Figure 9-12.

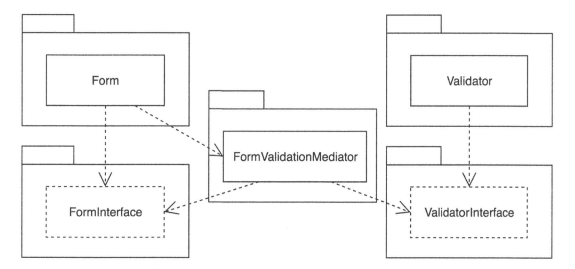

Figure 9-12. *Removing the dependency from ValidatorInterface to FormInterface by introducing another package to be the mediator between the two*

NAMING PATTERN-INSPIRED CLASSES

I think that FormValidationMediator is a bit of a strange class name, since it incorporates the name of the pattern that's been used. In my experience, it makes a lot more sense to name the class whatever is most appropriate in the context of your application and make sure it reads well. Then in the documentation of the class you could mention the pattern you've used and possibly why you've used it, if it may help the reader understand what's going on (as shown in Listing 9-16).

Listing 9-16. Using Documentation to Explain Which Design Pattern Has Been Used

```
/**
 * Mediator for validating Form objects using a generic
 * Validator object
 */
class FormValidation
{
    // ...
}
```

A mediator package is also known as a *bridge* package. A bridge connects two packages that will become more useful when used together, but shouldn't know about each other's existence or inner workings.

In some cases it even makes sense to call such a mediator package an *adapter* package. This would be the case if the mediator was defined inside the form package as an interface, e.g., `FormValidationMediatorInterface`. You could then create an adapter package containing an implementation of the `FormValidationMediatorInterface` using the particular validation library we've used in this example. Introducing the interface would also make it possible for users of the form package to use their own favorite validator by writing a single adapter class. This may remind you of a previous example involving the `HandlerInterface` from the `monolog` package, for which users could provide their own adapter implementation as well, and optionally distribute it as a package too.

Chain of Responsibility

Another useful pattern in our quest to break a dependency cycle is the *Chain of Responsibility*.[3] You can use it to allow other parts of the application to hook into a certain process and let them do whatever they like (see Listing 9-17).

---

[3]Erich Gamma e.a., *Design Patterns: Elements of Reusable Object-Oriented Software,* Addison-Wesley, 1994.

Listing 9-17. Using the Chain of Responsibility Pattern

```php
interface FormValidatorInterface
{
    public function validate(FormInterface $form);
}

class Form implements FormInterface
{
    private $validators = [];

    public function addValidator(
        FormValidatorInterface $validator
    ): void {
        $this->validators[] = $validator;
    }

    public function isValid(): bool
    {
        foreach ($this->validators as $validator) {
            $validator->validate($this);
        }

        // ...
    }
}
```

Any class implementing FormValidatorInterface can be added to the stack of validators. This is a nice example of applying the *Open/Closed* principle (Chapter 2) to the Form class. It is possible to change the behavior of the class with regard to validation by just injecting other objects into it, instead of modifying its code.

Please note that the original recipe for a *Chain of Responsibility* includes a separate object for the request and each of the candidates for this request needs to pass the request object to the next candidate explicitly. In most cases such an implementation is way too complex. A simple loop over the candidates makes much more sense and is definitely more readable too.

Using a chain of objects that have the same responsibility is a great way to decouple packages. The package may contain just one interface, which other packages can depend on (i.e., implement). The project that uses these packages then only needs to configure the object graph correctly. See Figure 9-13.

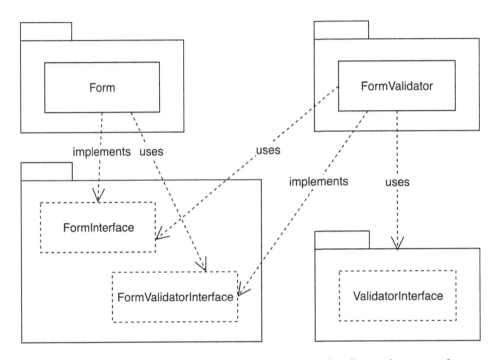

Figure 9-13. *A chain of responsibility used to break the dependency cycle*

Mediator and Chain of Responsibility Combined: An Event System

There's one last solution that's a very common and appropriate way of dissolving dependency cycles. It's a combination of a *Mediator* and a *Chain of Responsibility*. It is often known as an *event dispatcher* or an *event manager*.

An event dispatcher is an abstract mediator: the names and types of the messages are not predefined. It simply passes messages (events) to delegates (event listeners). In Listing 9-18, you will find a simple implementation of such an event dispatcher. It allows for event listeners (which should implement `ListenerInterface`) to be registered using the name of the event they want to listen to.

Listing 9-18. An EventDispatcher Implementation and the ListenerInterface

```php
class EventDispatcher
{
    private $listeners = [];

    public function registerListener(
        string $eventName,
        ListenerInterface $listener
    ): void {
        $this->listeners[$eventName][] = $listener;
    }

    public function dispatch(
        string $eventName,
        $eventData
    ): void {
        foreach ($this->getListeners($eventName) as $listener) {
            $listener->notify($eventData);
        }
    }

    private function getListeners($eventName): array
    {
        if (isset($this->listeners[$eventName])) {
            return $this->listeners[$eventName];
        }

        // no listeners are defined for this event
        return [];
    }
}

interface ListenerInterface
{
    public function notify($eventData): void;
}
```

In the Form class we can use the event dispatcher to trigger an event whenever the form has been submitted. Let's call this event form.submitted (see Listing 9-19).

Listing 9-19. Form Triggers an Event Upon Submission

```
class Form
{
    private $eventDispatcher;

    public function __construct(EventDispatcher $eventDispatcher)
    {
        $this->eventDispatcher = $eventDispatcher;
    }

    public function submit(array $data): void
    {
        // create the event object, provide the right context
        $event = new FormSubmittedEvent($this, $data);

        $this->eventDispatcher
            ->dispatch('form.submitted', $event);
    }

    // ...
}
```

The FormSubmittedEvent class is quite simple. It's only used to carry some contextual data about the event that occurred. In this case it allows event listeners to inspect (and modify) the form object itself and the data that was submitted (see Listing 9-20).

Listing 9-20. The Class of the Event That Gets Triggered Upon Form Submission

```
class FormSubmittedEvent
{
    private $form;

    public function __construct(FormInterface $form, array $data)
    {
        $this->form = $form;
    }

    public function getForm(): FormInterface
```

```
    {
        return $this->form;
    }

    public function getData(): array
    {
        return $this->data;
    }
}
```

Now we only need to implement an event listener that validates the form based on the submitted data. It listens to the `form.submitted` event and unpacks the `FormSubmittedEvent` object. When some of the submitted data from the event object is invalid, the listener adds an error to the form object (see Listing 9-21).

Listing 9-21. The Event Listener That Validates the Form's Data

```
class ValidateDataOnFormSubmitListener
{
    public function __construct(ValidatorInterface $validator)
    {
        $this->validator = $validator;
    }

    public function notify(FormSubmittedEvent $event): void
    {
        $form = $event->getForm();
        $submittedData = $event->getData();

        if (!$this->validator->validate(...)) {
            // part of the submitted data is invalid
            $form->addError(...);
        }
    }
}
```

To make all of this work, you need to set up the event dispatcher and register the form validation listener, then provide the event dispatcher as the constructor argument of the Form object (see Listing 9-22).

Listing 9-22. Setting Up the Event Dispatcher, Listener, and Form

```
$eventDispatcher = new EventDispatcher();
$validationListener = new ValidateDataOnFormSubmitListener();
$eventDispatcher->registerListener(
    'form.submitted',
    $validationListener
);

$form = new Form($eventDispatcher);

// will trigger the event listener
$form->submit([...]);
```

The EventDispatcher is a proper *mediator*: a Form never talks to a Validator directly, but always by means of the EventDispatcher. Inside the EventDispatcher, the listeners form a *Chain of Responsibility*. Each of them gets a chance to respond to the form.submitted event.

Looking at the dependency diagram (see Figure 9-14), we see no circles.

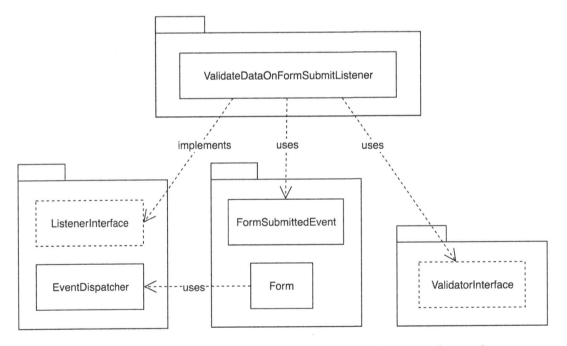

Figure 9-14. *The new dependency diagram, including the event dispatcher*

Maybe you're missing a connection between the event dispatcher and the event listener in this diagram. In a sense, the `EventDispatcher` should depend on the `ValidateDataOnFormSubmitListener` class. However, this is only a runtime dependency. If we look at the code there is no *strict* dependency on the `ValidateDataOnFormSubmitListener` class. You can use the `EventDispatcher` class without this particular event listener. Hence it should not result in a dependency between packages.

Using events to decouple packages can be very effective. However, there are also some disadvantages to doing so. First of all, an event dispatcher is a *highly abstract mediator*. There's nothing about the call to `EventDispatcher::dispatch()` that tells you that validation is going to happen. At the same time, validation is a concept that's very central to handling forms, so dealing with it behind the scenes in some event listener may not be the best solution. The better solution in this case would be to use dependency inversion. Introduce a `FormValidatorInterface` and have an adapter package with an implementation of this interface that knows how to use the `Validator` class. This will effectively remove the cyclic dependency.

There are other situations where using an event subsystem would be a smart solution though. For example, when you want to allow users to be notified when a process enters or leaves a certain phase. In that case, always aim to model the events themselves to be immutable. This should prevent hard-to-debug issues related to state that get modified in surprising ways inside event listeners.

If you do consider allowing event listeners to modify event data, see if you could instead use something like a filter or pipe mechanism. This allows you to stay away from the abstractness of the name "event dispatcher" and introduce some more meaningful class/interface names, like "form data filter," "request preprocessor," "response header collector," etc.

Conclusion

In this chapter we discussed many aspects of coupling. First we looked at different types of dependencies between classes, which can lead to package dependencies when the dependency of one class on another transcends the boundary of the package that contains the class.

When following the path from dependency to dependency, you sometimes return to the package from which you started. In that case, you have a cycle in your dependency graph. The *Acyclic Dependencies* principle told us not to have cycles in our dependency graph. Thinking about this, we concluded that cycles indeed cause a lot of trouble and, toward the end of this chapter, we learned that they are also not that hard to overcome.

Breaking all the cycles in our dependency graph (which is then an *acyclic directed graph*) makes it possible for us to easily create branches in the history of the packages. This means we can work on new minor and even major versions of a package, without preventing other packages from making progress or ever releasing their next major version at all. Having no cycles means that a change in one package affects only the smallest number of packages possible.

Being susceptible to changes in other packages, or necessitating other packages to change when your package changes, is the subject of the following two chapters.

CHAPTER 10

The Stable Dependencies Principle

In the previous chapter, we discussed the *Acyclic Dependencies* principle, which helps us prevent cycles in our dependency graphs. The greatest danger of cyclic dependencies is that problems in one of your dependencies might backfire after they have travelled the entire cycle through the dependency graph.

Even when your dependency graph has no cycles, there's still a chance that dependencies of a package will start causing problems at any time in the future. Whenever you upgrade one of your project's dependencies, you hope that your project will still work as it did before. However there's always the risk that it suddenly starts to fail in unexpected ways.

When your project still works after an upgrade of its dependencies, the maintainers of those dependencies are probably aware that many packages *depend on their package*. So in each patch or minor release, they will only fix bugs or add new features. They never push changes that would cause failure in a dependent package.

If, however, something is suddenly broken in your project after an upgrade of one of the dependencies, its package maintainers apparently made some changes that are not backward compatible. These kinds of changes bubble up through the dependency graph and cause problems in dependent packages.

When a dependency of your project suddenly causes failures, you must first rethink your choice of dependencies instead of blaming the maintainers. Some packages are highly volatile, some are not. It can be in the nature of a package to change frequently, for any reason. Maybe those changes are related to the problem domain, or maybe they are related to one of its dependencies.

Likewise, before adding a dependency to your project, you need to decide: is it likely that this dependency is going to change? Is it *easy* for its maintainers to change it? In other words, can the dependency be considered *stable*, or is it *unstable*?

© Matthias Noback 2018
M. Noback, *Principles of Package Design*, https://doi.org/10.1007/978-1-4842-4119-6_10

SEMANTIC VERSIONING AND STABILITY

As we discussed in the chapter about the *Release/Reuse Equivalence* principle (Chapter 6), the word "stable" is also used in the context of semantic versioning. A package is considered stable if it has a version that is at least 1.0.0, and is not in a development (or alpha, beta, RC) branch. Such a stable version promises to have a public API that does not change in backward incompatible ways.

The *Stable Dependencies* principle is also about the stability of a package, but isn't necessarily related to semantic versioning. In this chapter, "stable" means "not likely to change". A stable package in this context is a package on which many other packages depend, while it does not depend on other packages itself.

Stability

The stability of a package is all about how easy it is to change something in its code. This is not about clean code, or if the code can be easily refactored. It is about how *responsible* the package is with respect to other packages and if the package is susceptible to changes in any one of its dependencies.

Changes in the dependencies of a package are likely to bubble up to the package itself. You will often need to make changes to your own package to accommodate for changes in its dependencies. If you have a lot of dependencies, it's much more likely that an update of your dependencies will require you to modify your own package. Such a package would be called a *dependent package* (see Figure 10-1). When a package needs to be changed often to accommodate a change in one of its dependencies, it should be considered an *unstable* package.

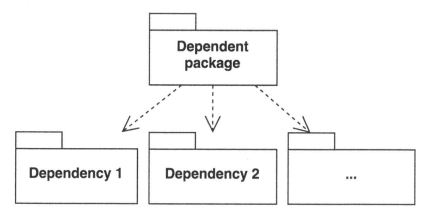

Figure 10-1. *A highly dependent package*

If a package has no dependencies, or just a small number of them, chances are that an update of your dependencies will cause no problems at all. Such a package is called an *independent package* (see Figure 10-2). Such a package isn't very susceptible to changes in its dependencies, so it should be considered a *stable* package.

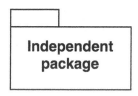

Figure 10-2. *An independent package*

There's another direction in the dependency graph that needs to be considered: the direction *toward* a package. In other words, how many other packages depend on a given package? If the number is high, it will be difficult to make changes to the package, because so many other packages are depending on it, and those local changes may require many modifications *elsewhere.* Such a package is called a *responsible package* (see Figure 10-3).

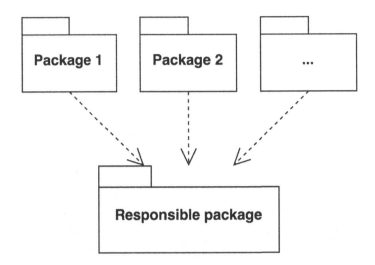

Figure 10-3. *A responsible package is a package that has many packages depending on it*

On the other hand, if the number of incoming dependencies is low or even lacking, it will be very easy for the package maintainer to make changes to it, since those changes will have little impact on other packages. We call a package with no other packages depending on it an *irresponsible package,* because it will not be held responsible for any changes that are made to it (see Figure 10-4).

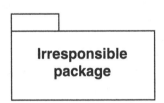

Figure 10-4. *An irresponsible package with no packages depending on it*

The maintainer of such an irresponsible package is free to change anything they like. On the contrary, a package with many dependents can be called *responsible* since its maintainer cannot just change anything they want. Any change should be expected to have an impact on depending packages.

At this point, it makes sense to not only take into account the number of packages depending on your package, but to also consider the number of applications that are depending on the package. As a package developer, you can't always get an accurate view of this, but package managers usually track the number of downloads for a package. If it's high, you can be certain that the package has many users. In that case, you have a responsible package, meaning that it needs to be stable for its users.

Not Every Package Can Be Highly Stable

Packages that are more independent and responsible should be considered *highly stable*. Those are packages that don't need to change because of a change in one of their dependencies, but they also can't easily change themselves because other packages heavily depend on them. See Figure 10-5.

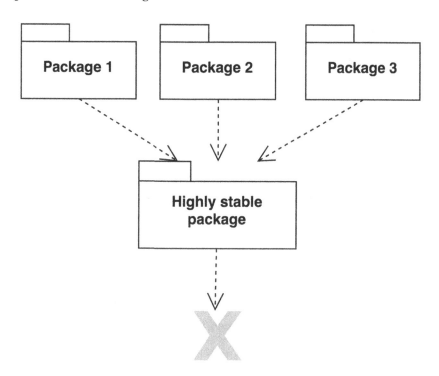

Figure 10-5. *A highly stable package: no dependencies, only dependents*

These highly stable packages are usually small libraries of code that implement some abstract concepts that are useful in many different contexts.

On the other side of the scale, packages that are more dependent but at the same time very irresponsible should be considered *highly unstable*. These packages are susceptible to changes in any of their dependencies, but they are not depended on by any other package, so it is no problem for them to change because a change would not ripple through. See Figure 10-6.

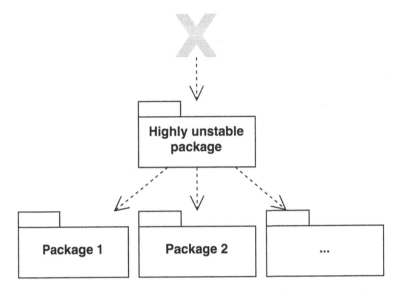

Figure 10-6. *A highly unstable package: many dependencies, no dependents*

These highly unstable packages are likely to contain concrete implementations that are, for example, coupled to a specific persistence library, or they may contain detailed implementations of business rules that are liable to change. Code that is only useful in the context of a certain application framework is also likely to be inside an unstable package, since a framework is itself highly unstable according to the definition used in this chapter.

Finally, there are packages that have no dependencies, but no other packages (or applications) depend on them too. These packages are independent and irresponsible. These are useless packages. Most packages, however, are somewhere between *highly independent and responsible* and *highly dependent and irresponsible*.

Unstable Packages Should Only Depend on More Stable Packages

Intuitively it would be alright for an unstable package to depend on a stable package. After all, the stable package is unlikely to have negative effects on an already unstable package. However, the other way around—a *stable* package that depends on an *unstable* package—would not be acceptable. The volatility of an unstable package would pose a threat to the stability of the stable package and would in fact make it less stable.

To prevent package designers from introducing "bad" dependencies, the *Stable Dependencies* principle tells us that:

> *The dependencies between packages in a design should be in the direction of the stability of the packages. A package should only depend upon packages that are more stable than it is.*[1]

In other words, less stable packages may depend on more stable packages. Stable packages should not depend on unstable packages.

Measuring Stability

Stability is actually a quantifiable unit, which we can use to determine if any package in a dependency graph satisfies the *Stable Dependencies* principle.

The conventional way of expressing stability is by calculating the I metric for packages. First you need to count the number of classes *outside* a package that depend on a class *inside* the package. We call this value C-in. Then you need to count the number of classes *outside* the package that any class *inside* the package depends on. We call this C-out.

You can then determine the I metric for the package by calculating C-out divided by C-in + C-out. This means that I will be between 0 and 1, where 1 indicates that the package is maximally unstable and 0 indicates that it is maximally stable.

A highly *stable* package is *responsible*: it has many dependents, so C-in is a high number. At the same time it's *independent*: it has no dependencies, so C-out = 0. This means that I = 0 since C-out / (C-in + C-out) = 0.

A highly *unstable* package is very *dependent*: it has many dependencies, so C-out is a high number. But it's also *irresponsible*: it has no other packages depending on it, so C-in = 0. Then I = 1 since C-out / (C-in + C-out) = 1.

Of course, these are very extreme examples. Most packages have an I that is not 0 nor 1, but somewhere in between. For example, the package in the center of

---

[1]Robert C. Martin, Engineering Notebook, C++ Report, Feb 1997 (PDF available on http://butunclebob.com/ArticleS.UncleBob.PrinciplesOfOod).

Figure 10-7 has a C-out of 3 and a C-in of 2, so the value of I for that package is 3 / (2 + 3) = 0.6. This means that the package should be considered relatively unstable; the number of outgoing dependencies is higher than the number of incoming dependencies.

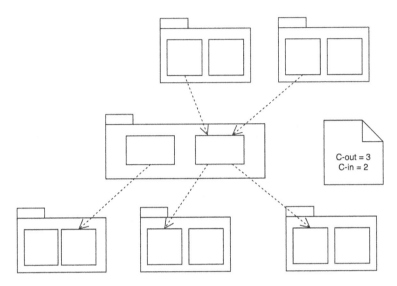

Figure 10-7. *Calculating C-in and C-out for the package in the center*

Decreasing Instability, Increasing Stability

According to the *Stable Dependencies* principle, the dependencies between packages in a design should be "in the direction of the stability of the packages". In other words, each step we take in the dependency graph should lead to a more stable package. More stable also means less unstable, so we are only allowed to take steps in the dependency graph leading to packages with a *lower* value for I (see Figure 10-8).

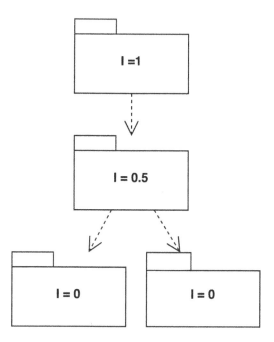

Figure 10-8. *An example of packages that all depend in the direction of stability*

When you draw such a diagram for your packages it's useful to put packages with a low I near the bottom and packages with a high I near the top. Then every dependency arrow should point downward since that is the direction of stability. If an arrow would point upward, like in Figure 10-9, the *Stable Dependencies* principle has been violated (we will later discuss your options to force the arrow in the right direction again).

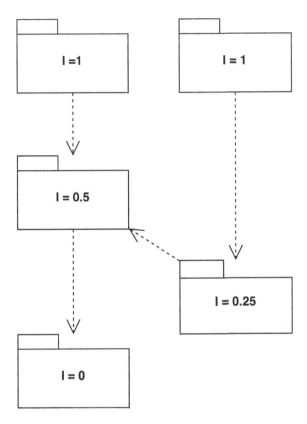

Figure 10-9. *An example of packages that do not all depend in the direction of stability*

Question: Should We Take Into Account All the Packages in the Universe?

It's an interesting question. The more packages that depend on a package, the more responsible that package will be, and therefore the more stable it becomes. But when calculating package coupling metrics, it would be practically impossible to take all the other packages and applications in the world into consideration. So, when we do calculate the I metric, and later the A metric, we can and should only look at all the packages that are installed in a given application. We can put them all into one big dependency diagram, and start verifying how well they follow the package coupling principles.

In the following sections, we discuss some violations of the *Stable Dependencies* principle and how you can fix them (if you have the power to do so!).

Violation: Your Stable Package Depends on a Third-Party Unstable Package

In the following example, I use the Gaufrette library,[2] which offers an abstraction layer for filesystems. It allows you to switch from a local filesystem to an in-memory filesystem, or even to Dropbox or Amazon storage, without the need to make changes to your own code.

The FileCopy class in Listing 10-1 is part of my own package. Its naive implementation of a copy mechanism allows you to copy files between any two filesystems. It depends on the Filesystem class offered by the Gaufrette library.

Listing 10-1. The FileCopy Class

```
use Gaufrette\Filesystem as GaufretteFilesystem

class FileCopy
{
    private $source;
    private $target;

    public function __construct(
        GaufretteFilesystem $source,
        GaufretteFilesystem $target
    ) {
        $this->source = $source;
        $this->target = $target;
    }

    public function copy($filename)
    {
        $fileContents = $this->source->get($filename);

        $this->target->write($filename, $fileContents);
    }
}
```

---

[2]https://github.com/KnpLabs/Gaufrette

The package that contains the FileCopy class, let's call it filesystem-manipulation, has an explicit dependency on the knplabs/gaufrette package that contains the Filesystem class, as shown in Listing 10-2.

Listing 10-2. List of Dependencies of the filesystem-manipulation Package

```
{
    "name": "filesystem-manipulation",
    "require": {
        "knplabs/gaufrette": "~0.1"
    }
}
```

Currently, FileCopy is the only class in this package. It has one dependency on a class of another package, which causes the C-out of this package to be 1. In the project in which the filesystem-manipulation package is being used, there is one class that uses the FileCopy class, so C-in is also 1, which causes I to be 1 / (1 + 1) = 0.5.

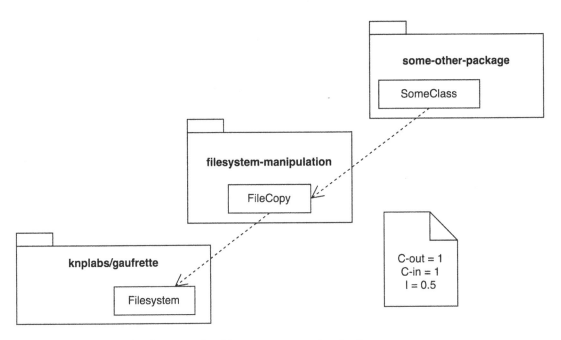

Figure 10-10. *Calculating I for filesystem-manipulation*

When we make the same calculation for the knplabs/gaufrette package, we need to count the number of classes outside that package that are depended on by classes inside the package. This package contains lots of adapter classes to make its filesystem abstraction work with all kinds of external storage solutions. All of these classes need extra dependencies to do the work. So this explains the high number of outgoing dependencies, which after counting turns out to be 54. So C-out = 54. Within the current project, only the FileCopy class depends on one of the classes of knplabs/gaufrette, so C-in = 1. This results in a fairly high value for I, namely 54 / (54 + 1) = 54/55, which is almost 1.

So knplabs/gaufrette turns out to be a *highly unstable* package. Much more unstable than our own filesystem-manipulation package. Nevertheless, the filesystem-manipulation package depends on the entire knplabs/gaufrette package. So we clearly violate the *Stable Dependencies* principle, since our packages do not all depend in the direction of stability. Instead, our package depends in the direction of *instability*. This becomes even more clear when we order the packages according to their stability and then draw the dependency arrows (see Figure 10-11).

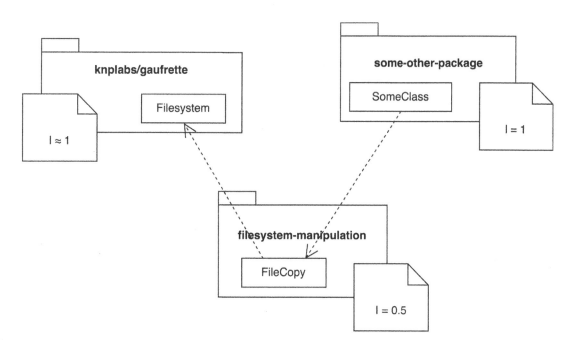

Figure 10-11. *The filesystem-manipulation package depends on a less stable package*

The reason why `knplabs/gaufrette` is such an unstable package is that it contains many concrete filesystem adapters for Dropbox, Amazon S3, SFTP, etc. These adapters are not used by everyone at the same time. So, according to the *Common Reuse* principle, they should have been in separate packages.

The `filesystem-manipulation` package does not need all those specific filesystem adapters; it only needs the `Filesystem` class, which provides generic methods for communicating with any specific filesystem.

Solution: Use Dependency Inversion

In order to fix the dependency graph and force the arrows to point in the direction of stability, we would very much like to take the `Filesystem` class (which is the *actual* filesystem abstraction layer) and put it inside a separate package: `knplabs/gaufrette-filesystem-abstraction`. Then the adapter classes should be placed inside other packages, like `knplabs/gaufrette-amazon-adapter`, `knplabs-/gaufrette-sftp-adapter`, etc. We could then change the dependency on `knplabs/gaufrette` to `knplabs/gaufrette-filesystem-abstraction` and this would do the trick.

However, we can't do this, since we are not the maintainers of `knplabs/gaufrette`. So we need to resort to another solution, one which we've already discussed: we should apply the *Dependency Inversion* principle. First, instead of depending on the `Gaufrette\Filesystem` class, which is still inside a highly unstable package, we define our own `FilesystemInterface` (see Listing 10-3) inside our `filesystem-manipulation` package.

Listing 10-3. The FilesystemInterface

```
interface FilesystemInterface
{
    public function read($path): string;

    public function write($path, $contents): void;
}
```

Then we let the constructor of `FileCopy` accept objects that implement this new `FilesystemInterface` (see Listing 10-4).

Listing 10-4. FileCopy Uses the New FilesystemInterface

```
class FileCopy
{
    // ...

    public function __construct(
        FilesystemInterface $source,
        FilesystemInterface $target
    ) {
        // ...
    }

    // ...
}
```

Now we can actually remove the dependency on knplabs/gaufrette from the package definition of our filesystem-manipulation package. As a matter of fact, the package has become independent at once: it has no dependencies at all. This means that it now has an I of 0 and it is to be considered highly stable.

As already mentioned, we'd still want to make use of the Gaufrette library. Therefore, we need to bridge the gap between FilesystemInterface and the Gaufrette\Filesystem class. We may accomplish this by introducing a new class, called GaufretteFilesystemAdapter (see Listing 10-5).

Listing 10-5. The GaufretteFilesystemAdapter

```
use Gaufrette\Filesystem as GaufretteFilesystem;

class GaufretteFilesystemAdapter implements FilesystemInterface
{
    private $gaufretteFilesystem;

    public function __construct(
        GaufretteFilesystem $gaufretteFilesystem
    ) {
        $this->gaufretteFilesystem = $gaufretteFilesystem;
    }
```

```
public function read($path): string
{
    return $this->gaufretteFilesystem->get($path);
}

public function write($path, $contents): void
{
    $this->gaufretteFilesystem->write($path, $contents);
}
}
```

This class uses Gaufrette's filesystem object by composition and is at the same time a proper substitute for FilesystemInterface. We put this class in a new package, called gaufrettefilesystem-adapter. Since the class needs both the FilesystemInterface and the Gaufrette\Filesystem class, it depends on both knplabs/gaufrette and filesystem-manipulation (see Listing 10-6).

Listing 10-6. List of Dependencies of the gaufrette-filesystem-adapter Package

```
{
    "name": "gaufrette-filesystem-adapter",
    "require": {
        "knplabs/gaufrette": "1.*"
        "filesystem-manipulation": "*"
    }
}
```

The C-out of this new gaufrette-filesystem-adapter package is 2, because it uses two classes outside the package. Its C-in is 0, since no other package uses a class from this package. This means I = 2 /(2 + 0) = 1. It's highly unstable (i.e., easy to change), which is totally fine for an adapter package.

Take a look at Figure 10-12 to find out what all this did for the dependency graph and the arrows in it.

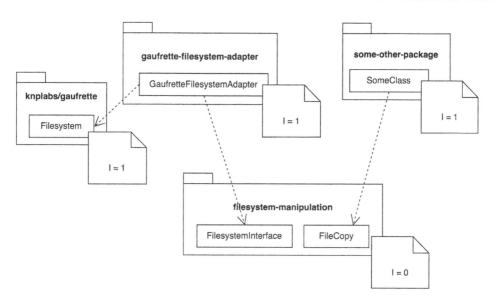

Figure 10-12. *Each package depends in the direction of stability*

The packages are now sorted in the direction of stability, and all dependency arrows are pointing downward, which means that no package in this system violates the *Stable Dependencies* principle anymore.

All of this was accomplished without making any changes to third-party code. We applied the *Dependency Inversion* principle to the `FileCopy` class by letting it depend on something abstract instead of something concrete. This automatically makes the `FileCopy` class easily extensible: others can implement their own adapters for `Filesystem` and make it compatible with, for instance, the `Flysystem` filesystem abstraction library.[3] It also makes the `filesystem-manipulation` better maintainable, since changes in `knplabs/gaufrette` will not affect it anymore.

Staying unaffected by external changes makes the `filesystem-manipulation` package very stable. It's unlikely to change because of its dependencies (since it has no dependencies anymore). Its previous instability is pushed away to the more concrete `gaufrette-filesystem-adapter` package, which is now susceptible to changes in `knplabs/gaufrette`. But even though the code inside the `gaufrette-filesystem-adapter` package is likely to change, it poses no threat to other parts of the system, since no other package depends on it.

---

[3]`https://github.com/thephpleague/flysystem`

A Package Can Be Both Responsible and Irresponsible

As I already quickly pointed out, the knplabs/gaufrette package has some design issues. It contains classes that would not be used by everyone who uses the package in their project, so it violates the *Common Reuse* principle. It also contains classes (the same classes actually) that are not closed against the same kinds of changes, so the package violates the *Common Closure* principle.

Now that we are looking at the knplabs/gaufrette package from the perspective of stability, it becomes clear that grouping those classes that actually don't belong together is the reason why this package has become very unstable. It introduces many external dependencies, which makes it no longer safe for other packages to depend on it.

Not being safe to depend on is not a good property for packages that are supposed to be highly reusable. In fact, a reliable package should be very safe to depend on: it should be stable. In other words, it should be independent and responsible.

In the previous section we discussed a solution for this stability problem. It entailed the introduction of an interface and an adapter to rearrange the dependency directions. We needed to resort to this solution because we could not do what was really necessary—to split the package into a package containing the more generally reusable parts (like the Gaufrette\Filesystem class and the Gaufrette\Adapter interface) and one or more packages containing the more specific and concrete parts (like the filesystem adapters for SFTP, Dropbox, etc.).

The first package would have no dependencies, only dependents, which would make it independent and responsible, i.e. very stable. We would call it knplabs/gaufrette-filesystem-abstraction. The other packages would be named after the specific filesystems they provided an implementation for, like knplabs/gaufrette-sftp-adapter. Each of those packages could then have as many dependencies as needed by the specific filesystem implementation. And of course each of them would depend on knplabs/gaufrette-filesystem-abstraction because that package will contain the interface that each filesystem adapter needs to implement. It would make those adapter packages dependent and a bit less irresponsible. That is, the number of package depending on it will be smaller than the number of packages and applications depending on the core filesystem abstraction package.

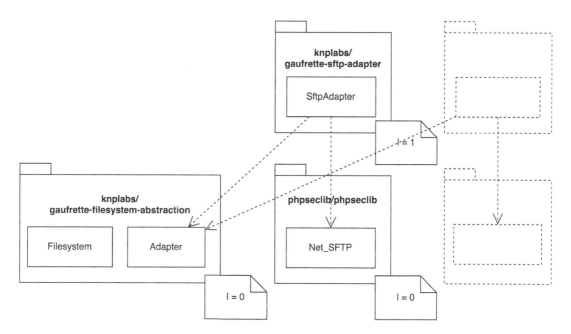

Figure 10-13. *knplabs/gaufrette-* packages after refactoring*

The great thing is that in such a constellation of packages, knplabs/gaufrette-filesystem-abstraction would be very stable, and the filesystem-manipulation package containing the FileCopy class could safely depend on it. The filesystem-manipulation package itself has an I of 0.5, while knplabs/gaufrette-filesystem-abstraction has an I of 0, which is lower. All package dependencies would follow the direction of stability, so the *Stable Dependencies* principle would not be violated.

Conclusion

According to the *Stable Dependencies* principle, packages should depend in the direction of stability. This means that every package should depend only on packages that are *more* stable than the package itself is. The stability of a package is a measurement of how likely it is to change.

A *stable* package will be both independent (it has only a few dependencies, or none at all) and responsible (many classes depend on it). An *unstable* package will be dependent (it has many dependencies) and irresponsible (no classes, or just a few, depend on it).

With the I-metric, (in)stability can be quantified as C-out / (C-out + C-in), where C-out is the number of classes the package depends on, and C-in is the number of classes that depend on a class in this package. If I gets closer to 1, the package is relatively unstable. If it gets closer to 0, it's relatively stable.

## CHAPTER 11

The Stable Abstractions Principle

We've reached the last of the design principles related to package coupling, which means we have in effect reached the last of *all* the package design principles. This principle, the *Stable Abstractions* principle, is about stability, just like the *Stable Dependencies* principle. While the previous principle told us to depend "in the direction of stability," this principle says that packages should depend in the direction of *abstractness*.

Stability and Abstractness

The name of the *Stable Abstractions* principle contains two important words: "stable" and "abstract". We already discussed stability of packages in the previous chapter. A stable package is not likely to change heavily. It has no dependencies so there is no external reason for it to change. At the same time, other packages depend on it. Therefore, the package should not change, in order to prevent problems with those depending packages.

In the previous chapter, we learned that you can calculate stability and that you can verify that the dependency graph of a project contains only dependencies of increasing stability, or decreasing instability. In this chapter, we learn that we also have to calculate the abstractness of packages and that the dependency direction should be one of increasing abstractness, or decreasing concreteness.

The concept of abstractness is something we also encountered in previous chapters. For example, in the chapter about the *Dependency Inversion* principle (Chapter 5), we learned that our classes should depend on abstractions, not on concretions.

© Matthias Noback 2018
M. Noback, *Principles of Package Design*, https://doi.org/10.1007/978-1-4842-4119-6_11

We discussed several ways in which a class can be abstract. The most obvious way is when a class has abstract (also known as virtual) methods. These methods have to be defined in a subclass. This subclass is a concrete class because it is a full implementation of the type of thing that the abstract class tries to model. When a class only has abstract methods, we usually don't call it a class, but an interface. Classes that implement the interface eventually have to provide an implementation for all of the abstract methods defined in the interface.

The *Dependency Inversion* principle told us to depend on abstractions, not on concretions. The reason was, like always, that we need to be prepared for change. A class that depends on a concrete thing is likely to change whenever some implementation detail of the concrete thing changes (see Figure 11-1). Besides, if at some point we want to replace the concrete thing with another concrete thing, we'd have to modify the class to understand and use that new concrete thing. And in that situation it's probably not the only class that needs to be modified.

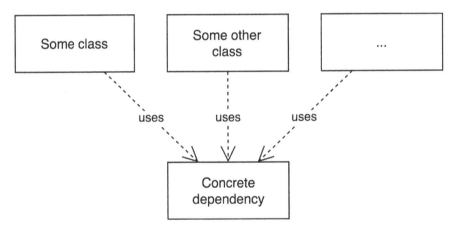

Figure 11-1. *Depending on concrete things*

If instead we define something abstract, like an abstract class or preferably an interface, and we depend on it, we are much better prepared for change (see Figure 11-2). Most changes occur in concrete things, i.e., in fully implemented classes. The abstract things, like interfaces, will remain the same over a longer period of time. So if we depend on an abstract thing, it is likely that we will not be negatively influenced by it—it's supposed to be very *stable*.

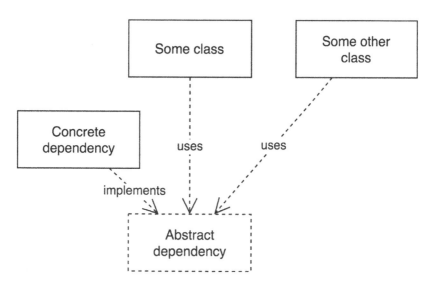

Figure 11-2. *Depending on abstract things*

And this is where the two concepts, stability and abstractness, meet. If we consider stability to be the likeliness that something is going to change, then what is true for classes is also true for packages. As we know now, it's better to depend on stable packages than to depend on unstable packages. Stable packages are less likely to change, so a depending package won't be negatively influenced by changes in its dependencies. In the same way it's safer to depend on abstract classes or interfaces because they are less likely to change.

We can follow the same reasoning while we apply the concept of abstractness to packages: it would be better to depend on an abstract package than on a concrete package. For the same reason—an abstract package would contain no particular implementation details that would be susceptible to change. Over a longer period of time it will stay the same.

How to Determine If a Package Is Abstract

The question is: is it possible to mark a package as either abstract or concrete? It is possible, even though "being abstract" is not a Boolean value. There are many degrees of abstractness. We might consider a class to be abstract if it contains *at least one abstract method*. Then a class is concrete if it has no abstract (or virtual) methods.

We can determine the abstractness of packages in a similar way. A package is abstract if it contains no regular classes, only interfaces and abstract classes. And a package is concrete if it has at least one fully implemented, concrete class.

Still we'd need a little nuance here. According to this definition of abstract and concrete packages, a package with 10 interfaces and 1 concrete class would count as a concrete package, even though it contains many more abstract things than concrete things. Therefore, we should take the total number of classes and interfaces into account.

The A Metric

The suggested way to find an indication of the abstractness of packages is to calculate the number of abstract classes and interfaces in a package, then divide that number by the total number of concrete classes, abstract classes, and interfaces in that package. The resulting thing would be a quotient with a value somewhere between 0 and 1. We call this number the A metric for packages:

```
A = C-abstract / (C-concrete + C-abstract)
```

When the value of the A metric for a package is equal to or near 0, it's a highly concrete package. It contains (almost) no interfaces, only concrete classes, so it's full of implementation details, and therefore liable to change.

When, on the other hand, the A metric is equal to or near 1, it's a highly abstract package. It contains (almost) no concrete classes, but mostly abstract classes and interfaces. It's likely that these abstract things will stay the same over time. After all, only concrete classes and consequently concrete packages are liable to change.

Abstract Things Belong in Stable Packages

So abstract packages are stable too. Or at least, they should be. This is where the *Stable Abstractions* principle steps in:

> *Packages that are maximally stable should be maximally abstract. Instable packages should be concrete. The abstraction of a package should be in proportion to its stability.[1]*

---

[1]Robert C. Martin, Engineering Notebook, C++ Report, Feb 1997 (PDF available on `http://butunclebob.com/ArticleS.UncleBob.PrinciplesOfOod`).

We already know that a package should depend only on packages that are more stable. Now we also know that abstract things are likely to be more stable, i.e., they change less often and less dramatically. Hence concrete classes can safely depend on them. But what if an interface is part of a highly unstable package? Then it's consequently not safe to depend on that package. The unstable package is likely to change. The interface inherits the instability of its containing package.

Interfaces and abstract classes are better off in a stable package. The stability of the package itself will be beneficial for the abstract things it contains. At the same time, the abstract things are good for the stability of the containing package. Packages that apply the *Dependency Inversion* principle start to depend on it because of the abstract things it contains. This turns it into a more responsible package and will thereby force it to become more stable.

The opposite is also true: concrete classes are better off in unstable packages. The implementation details of the classes are likely to change anyway and this would better happen in an unstable package, which has less responsibility toward depending packages. If, however, a concrete class would be inside a highly stable package, it would make that package more unstable because a concrete class is liable to change.

Abstractness Increases with Stability

The *Stable Abstractions* principle adds one extra requirement. It wants to unify abstractness and stability into this simple rule: a package should be as abstract as it is stable.

Let's assume you have a number of packages and have calculated the I values for all of them. Remember the I value indicates the stability of a package: the closer the value is to 1, the more unstable a package is. The closer it is to 0, the more stable it is. When you draw them in a diagram, the packages with the highest value for I are at the top and those with the lowest value for I are at the bottom. When you travel from a package to its dependencies you encounter packages that only have decreasing values for I (see Figure 11-3), that is, they become more and more stable.

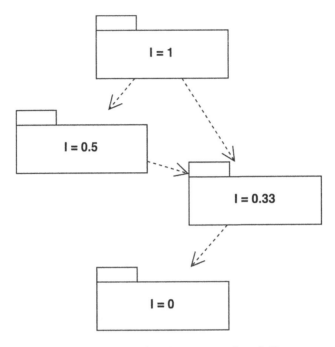

Figure 11-3. *All dependencies go in the direction of stability*

To figure out if you have also applied the *Stable Abstractions* principle correctly, you also need to calculate the values for A (by dividing the number of abstract classes and interfaces by the total number of classes and interfaces). Then add the resulting A values to the dependency diagram (see Figure 11-4).

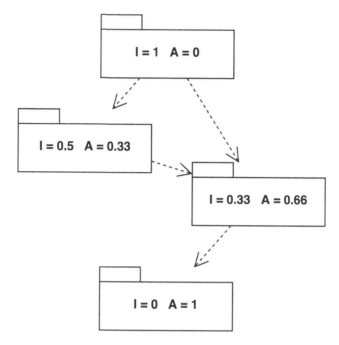

Figure 11-4. *All dependencies go in the direction of abstractness*

Now you only need to verify that each dependency arrow leads to a package with a higher value for A. In other words, dependencies should have an increasing abstractness.

Strictly speaking, the values for I and A added together should be exactly 1. This would mean that all packages are *as abstract as they are stable*. But this is completely unrealistic. There is always some margin to this. However, I + A should not be too far away from 1. In general, highly abstract packages should be highly stable, and concrete packages should be unstable.

The Main Sequence

It's possible that stable packages contain concrete classes and unstable packages contain abstract classes or interfaces. These packages might be easy to spot, but there are many degrees of stability and abstractness. To find out which packages have imbalanced values for I and A, we can plot the packages in a diagram called the *main sequence diagram.*

We first draw a vertical axis going from 0 to 1. It stands for the degree of *abstractness* of a package (expressed by A). Then we draw a horizontal axis going from 0 to 1.

This represents the degree of *instability* of a package (expressed by I). Finally, we draw a diagonal line from the top-left corner to the bottom-right corner. This line is called the *main sequence* (see Figure 11-5).

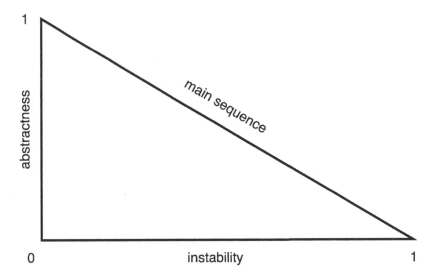

Figure 11-5. *The main sequence diagram template*

Now we plot each package at the right spot in the diagram, based on its values for I and A (see Figure 11-6).

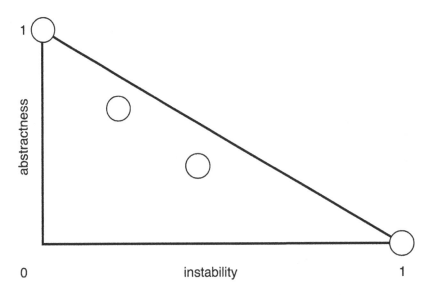

Figure 11-6. *The main sequence diagram for the packages in the previous dependency diagram*

244

You'll know when you have applied both the *Stable Dependencies* principle and the *Stable Abstractions* principle correctly if all the packages are near or on the diagonal, i.e. the main sequence. According to this rule, the previously shown main sequence diagram looks pretty good.

If you find any package that lies quite far from the main sequence, you should take a closer look at it. Consider its surrounding packages too and try to make some changes to its dependencies or its dependents in order to achieve the right amount of stability. It may also be necessary to change the abstractness of the package by relocating some abstract classes or interfaces.

Once you've fixed the biggest issues with stability and abstractness, you shouldn't forget to regularly come back to see if packages have not started to drift away from the main sequence. After some time the nature of existing packages may change because of new features being added to them and this may eventually cause an imbalance.

Types of Packages

When you travel down the main sequence from the top-left to the bottom-right corner, you will first come across highly *concrete, highly unstable packages*. These should all be application-level packages. They are full of implementation details, specific to the actual project you're working on. They are allowed to be concrete, because no other package depends on them. Hence, they are unstable packages bound to change as often as the business changes.

Taking some more steps on the main sequence you will find in the middle packages that are somewhat abstract and somewhat stable. They are much less affected by external changes, but to a certain degree they are allowed to change themselves without bringing the whole project in danger.

When the journey on the main sequence ends, you will be in the realm of *abstract, stable packages*: the foundational blocks of your application. These contain lots of interfaces and abstract classes, which is why many classes (and consequently packages) depend on them. These classes apply the *Dependency Inversion* principle correctly in order to be less susceptible to change. Hence, these abstract packages should be stable too. And they are, because they are responsible and have no dependencies themselves.

INTERFACE PACKAGES

When you want to create highly abstract, stable packages, you may end up simply extracting the interfaces from existing packages and putting them all in one big *interface package*.

This is not the best thing you can do for your project. By putting all the interfaces in one package, you are going to violate the *Common Reuse* principle: some clients need just one or two interfaces from the package, but still they would have to depend on the entire package.

Besides, not all interfaces are meant to be depended on outside of a given package. You may have lots of interfaces that are only for private use within the same package (depending on your programming language, you may be able to mark an interface as private).

One last thing to be aware of: before moving interfaces to a separate project, make sure that you have properly applied the *Interface Segregation* principle to all of them. That way, clients won't be forced to depend on interfaces with methods they do not or should not want to use.

If you properly apply these rules, go ahead and create lots of small interface packages, each in support of one specific feature.

Strange Packages

What happens in the corners that lie far away from the main sequence? What misbehaving packages can be found there (see Figure 11-7)?

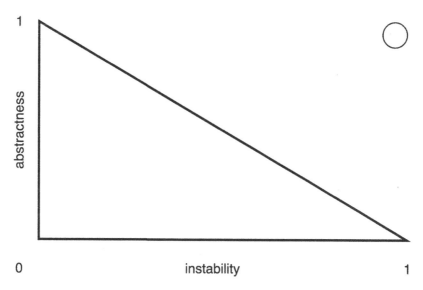

Figure 11-7. *A package in the top-right corner*

In the top-right corner, we will find packages that are both highly abstract and highly unstable. These packages can thus be characterized as:

- Irresponsible (no other packages depend on them)

- Dependent (they depend on lots of other packages)

- Abstract (they contain only abstract classes or interfaces)

This is a very strange kind of package. It's very unlikely that such a package can be found in your project, because it would most likely contain *dead code*. It's never used by any part of the project, yet the code is abstract, meaning that it cannot be used standalone—someone has to provide an implementation for it. In other words, packages like these are useless and you should try to get rid of them.

On the opposite side of the diagram, in the bottom-left corner (see Figure 11-8), you will find packages that are highly concrete, yet highly stable.

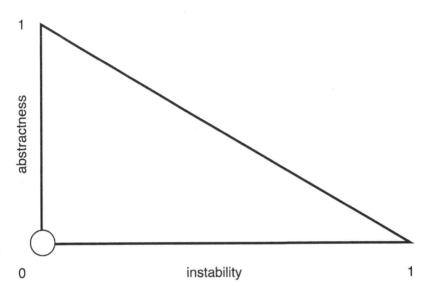

Figure 11-8. *A package in the bottom-left corner*

Such packages are:

- Responsible (many packages depend on them)
- Independent (they have no dependencies)
- Concrete (they contain only concrete classes)

This kind of package would be heavily used all over the project. Because it doesn't need any other packages to do its work, this is probably some kind of low-level library. However, it doesn't offer any abstractions for the things it does. This means that it's hard for classes in other packages to naturally comply to the *Dependency Inversion* principle: they have to depend on the concrete classes from this package instead of interfaces.

The solution for getting this package back in shape is to apply the *Dependency Inversion* principle to *depending* packages. They should not depend on the concrete classes from this package anymore, but instead depend on their own interfaces or interfaces defined in some more stable and abstract package.

Conclusion

In this chapter, we discussed the intimate relation between stability and abstractness. We learned that the more stable a package is, the more abstract things it should contain. The counterpart of this is that the more concrete things a package contains, the more unstable it becomes.

We looked at the main sequence diagram to get a grip on different kinds of packages and where they are on the sliding scale between concrete/unstable and abstract/stable. Using this diagram, we are able to spot packages with extraordinary characteristics.

## CHAPTER 12

Conclusion

Now that we have discussed so many design principles, you may feel that it's time to get a little bit more practical. You just want to finally start creating wonderful packages and share them with your co-workers, or even with the international open source software audience. I definitely think you should do that. Before you do, I want to give you some last words of advice.

Creating Packages Is Hard

In his book, *Facts and Fallacies of Software Engineering*, Robert Glass mentions some interesting "facts" about reusable software components (or "packages"). First of all:

> *Reuse-in-the-small (libraries of subroutines) [...] is a well-solved problem.*[1]

Reuse-in-the-Small

There are all kinds of little shared functions that are very useful and help you quickly solve ever-recurring problems, like sorting an array, reading bytes from a file, etc. These are often distributed as "standard libraries" along with the runtime of your programming language.

By combining basic functions like these, you can produce some new low-level functions. As long as these functions are sufficiently small and unspecific, there should be no problem in reusing them in other projects. You only have to make sure that you release the code properly.

---

[1]Robert L. Glass, *Facts and Fallacies of Software Engineering*, Pearson Education, 2003.

© Matthias Noback 2018
M. Noback, *Principles of Package Design*, https://doi.org/10.1007/978-1-4842-4119-6_12

Reuse-in-the-Large

When we keep combining and restructuring these low-level functions, we eventually produce complex and advanced software components. If you want to *reuse* entire software components in other projects, that's a whole different story. As Glass puts it:

> *Reuse-in-the-large (components) remains a mostly unsolved problem [...].*[2]

It's much harder to prepare these bigger components for reuse than it is to write small, reusable functions. The main reason is that components usually fulfill an application-specific goal. Most components in a project are the result of actual requirements for that project.

Even though there are still lots of projects in the world that share some or a big part of their requirements (probably because they are part of the same business domain), no two applications are the same. This means that there is always some aspect of a component that wouldn't be useful in another project, or that would contradict some of the other project's requirements, etc.

When you're working on a component that you want to make reusable, it can be very hard, maybe impossible, to think of all the ways in which other developers might want to use it. Often you recognize room for improvement only after someone points it out to you.

Embracing Software Diversity

Glass attributes the fact that reuse-in-the-large is so hard to something called *software diversity*:

> *If, as many suspect, the diversity of applications and domains means that no two problems are very similar to one another, then only those common housekeeping functions and tasks are likely to be generalized.*[3]

Creating reusable components (or "packages") may be possible only if:

- The domain of two projects is the same

or

- The component offers general-purpose functionality

---

[2]Robert L. Glass, *Facts and Fallacies of Software Engineering,* Pearson Education, 2003.
[3]Robert L. Glass, *Facts and Fallacies of Software Engineering,* Pearson Education, 2003.

In the first case, components model some part of the shared domain in a reusable way, leaving some details to the client. For example, it may be possible to reuse an online payment component in several e-commerce applications. Or, if you write flight control software like NASA does, you will likely be able to reuse some components in the next project. As Robert Glass mentions, NASA reports the amount of code reuse to be around 70%, which should be mainly attributed to the fact that most of their projects have a shared problem domain.

In the second case, components offer some generally useful features, like logging things, talking to a server over HTTP, processing web requests, converting Markdown to HTML, etc. These types of things are useful in large subsets of all applications. As long as they offer lots of configuration options and apply the SOLID and package design principles correctly, these components or packages have a good chance of being easily reusable.

Component Reuse Is Possible, But Requires More Work

When you intend your code to be reusable, you should be constantly concerned with extensibility, readability, automated tests, code quality, etc. If you want your reusable code to be successful in lots of projects, you should be aware of any environmental differences between those projects (different versions of the programming language, different operating systems, etc.). You have to provide some level of care for the package, like offering support or providing bug fixes. You need to offer some kind of a product experience, e.g. by writing a bit of documentation and providing usage examples. All of the effort you put into it leads to the following rule of thumb, as proposed by Glass:

> *It is three times as difficult to build reusable components as single use components [...].*[4]

After all of that, you would still be in the position where *only you* have used the component in a project. You don't know yet how it will behave in other projects, if it will live up to any other developer's expectations. Therefore a second rule of thumb is introduced:

> *[...] a reusable component should be tried out in three different applications before it will be sufficiently general to accept into a reuse library.*[5]

---

[4]Robert L. Glass, *Facts and Fallacies of Software Engineering*, Pearson Education, 2003.
[5]Robert L. Glass, *Facts and Fallacies of Software Engineering*, Pearson Education, 2003.

Creating Packages Is Doable

I agree with the first rule of thumb. In my experience creating reusable software takes definitely more time than creating non-reusable software. I don't know exactly how much more, but three times more sounds about right. However, you can certainly influence this amount of time (and effort) by considering these factors:

- The number of features that your package provides

- The area of the domain that your package covers

- The level of extensibility of your package

Reducing the Impact of the First Rule of Three

If your package has too many features because you want to satisfy a group of users that is as large as possible, it's likely that you will spend ever-increasing amounts of time on maintaining that package. All those features will start to get in each other's way. Fixing a bug in one feature might break another feature. Besides, each of those features has its own dependencies, which makes the package quite unstable.

If your package tries to cover a big area of the problem domain, you will most likely be spending lots of time trying to implement all imaginable details that *can* be part of the domain. A business domain usually has so many aspects that may be slightly or even largely different for distinct projects in the same domain that it's impossible to cover them all with your package. Users of your package will always be able to point out some more details that you overlooked.

These two factors for the amount of time and effort required to create a package are both related to the *scope of the package*. Our conclusion based on these discussions should be that we *always need to limit scope*.

There is one other thing that we need to do in order to influence the amount of time that we need to invest: we need to make sure that our packages are highly extensible. If users of a package are not able to change the behavior of its classes without modifying or overriding the actual code, they will come to you to complain about that. Instead of asking *you* to add that one feature they're missing, you should enable them to add that feature *themselves*. This should save you a lot of time and make your package very attractive to its users.

Reducing the Impact of the Second Rule of Three

The second rule of three stated that we should try our reusable component out in at least three different applications. In my experience, this isn't always necessary. Whether or not to follow this rule depends on the situation, though.

Do you consider sharing the code with the world? Then you may as well ship it right away and find out what will happen. Of course, it helps to imagine potential use cases and accommodate the code to enable those. But there will always be one edge case you didn't think of. Releasing a package with a license that provides no guarantees to the users can be a great way to get feedback that shows you how reusable your code really is.

Maybe you don't intend to open source your code, but you want to reuse it in different applications of your own making. Then you shouldn't immediately put the code in a package, but simply copy it over to the next project and see if it proves its usefulness there.

The reason to make this distinction is that there's a significant cost involved in packaging code. As you know, applying the *Release/Reuse Equivalence* principle to packages can provide you with a lot of extra work. You don't know yet if all this work is going to pay off. If you've used the code in only one project, you don't know yet if it's actually reusable. First you need to find out if the code deserves packaging by seeing how well it adapts to a second project. That's also why you shouldn't immediately aim for reusability of any piece of code you write for a project. Only when you experience the need for this code in a second project, and possibly a third, you should consider packaging it.

An application is usually better off with code that is specific to the project and its domain. Always aiming for abstract and generic solutions is an interesting programming exercise, but the project and its developers are better off with code that recognizably matches the expected behavior of the application, and the concepts of the application's problem domain. That's why it isn't smart to always write code with potential reusability in mind.

Once you spot a couple of classes that show some potential for being reusable, you can always move those classes to a separate directory/namespace within the project and see if they are viable as a standalone component. It will be a good incentive to improve the design of those classes, and to hide some logic behind a *Façade* or interface provided by the component. In practice though, I've found that the vast majority of the code that I wrote in this a manner never ended up in an actual package.

On the other hand, looking at my own experiences as a package developer, some packages turn out to be very useful for others. My personal return-on-investment in terms of time spent versus time saved isn't always that favorable (on the contrary I'd say). Nevertheless, it's great to see that releasing code that I thought should've been publicly available indeed turned out to be useful for others.

Creating Packages Is Easy?

In the previous sections we changed our mind from "creating packages is hard" to "creating packages is doable". Could we take the next step and conclude that creating packages is *easy*? On the one hand, yes, I think that it can be very easy. When you make a habit of following good class design practices, writing clean code and testing your code before or while you're writing it, you'll find that it isn't hard to pick up that code and distribute it as a package.

On the other hand, if you start with concrete, single use-case, project-specific code, and no quality assurance measurements in place, it can be very hard as well to create a reusable package from that. In that case, I'd say you will have a hard time maintaining that code anyway.

So in general my advice is to write code in the best way you can. That way, if you ever want to make it reusable, it will be a goal you can achieve. And if you don't, you will have a good time maintaining it. Write your code well, and you will always be better off.

APPENDIX A

The Full Page Class

```php
<?php
class Page
{
  public $uri = null;
  public $assigns = array();
  public $page = array();
  public $parent_node = 0;
  public $site_title = '';
  public $breadcrumbs = array();
  public $auto_include_dir = '';
  /* @public $smart Smarty */
  public $smarty = null;
  public $default_template = '';
  public $template = '';
  public $cms_login = null;
  public $user_login = null;
  public $available = true;
  public $is_user = false;
  public $is_admin = false;
  public $menu_items = array();
  public $caching = 1;
  public $cache_id = null;

  protected $_extra_request_parameters = array();

  /**
   * @param array $parameters
   */
```

© Matthias Noback 2018
M. Noback, *Principles of Package Design*, https://doi.org/10.1007/978-1-4842-4119-6

```php
public function setExtraRequestParameters(array $parameters)
{
  $this->_extra_request_parameters = array_values($parameters);
}

/**
 * @return array
 */
public function getExtraRequestParameters()
{
  return $this->_extra_request_parameters;
}

public function __construct($uri)
{
  $this->connect_db();
  header('Content-Type: '.HEADER_CONTENT_TYPE);
  $this->smarty = new Smarty;

  if (isset($_GET['clear_cache']))
  {
    $this->smarty->clear_cache();
  }

  if (DEBUGGING)
  {
    $this->smarty->caching = false;
    if (trusted_ip())
    {
      $this->smarty->debugging = true;
    }
  }

  if (trusted_ip())
  {
    ini_set('display_errors', '1');
    error_reporting(
```

```
    E_ERROR | E_PARSE | E_WARNING
    | E_USER_ERROR | E_USER_NOTICE | E_USER_WARNING);
}
else
{
  $this->smarty->debugging = false;
  ini_set('display_errors', '0');
  error_reporting(0);
}

$this->smarty->template_dir = ROOT.'/site/templates';
$this->smarty->compile_dir = ROOT.'/site/templates_c';
$this->smarty->use_sub_dirs = true;
$this->default_template = DEFAULT_TEMPLATE;

if (!table_exists('content'))
{
  require(ROOT.'/includes/install.php');
  install();
}

$this->add_title_part(SITE_TITLE);

$this->cms_login = new LoginClass('admins', 'cms_login');
$this->user_login = new LoginClass('users', 'user_login');

if ($this->cms_login->isLoggedIn())
{
  $this->is_admin = true;
}

if ($this->user_login->isLoggedIn())
{
  $this->is_user = true;
}
```

```
$parsed_url = parse_url($uri);
$relative = ROOT;
$url = $parsed_url['path'];
$this->assign('header_content_type', HEADER_CONTENT_TYPE);
$this->determine_page($url);
if ($this->smarty->is_cached(", 'page_'.$this->page['id']))
{
  $this->smarty->display(
    $this->default_template,
    'page_'.$this->page['id']);
  exit;
}

$this->smarty->register_function(
  'translate',
  'smarty_function_translate'
);
$this->smarty->register_modifier(
  'translate',
  'smarty_modifier_translate'
);
$this->smarty->register_function(
  'url_for',
  'smarty_function_url_for'
);

$this->open_page();
}

function get_page_info($id)
{
  $result = mysql_query(
    "SELECT c.id, c.uri, t.title, t.menu_name, " .
    "c.node, c.skip_to_first_subpage FROM content c " .
    "WHERE c.id='$id';"
  );
```

```php
  if ($result && mysql_num_rows($result))
  {
    return mysql_fetch_assoc($result);
  }
  return false;
}

function determine_page($url)
{
  $url_parts = explode('/', trim($url, '/'));

  $page_ids = array();
  $uri_prefix = ";
  $parent_id = 0;

  foreach($url_parts as $key => $part)
  {
    if ($key == 0 || empty($part))
    {
      unset($url_parts[$key]);

      continue;
    }

    $result = mysql_query("SELECT id, skip_to_first_subpage ".
      "FROM content c WHERE t.uri='".addslashes($part)."' ".
      "AND c.parent_id='$parent_id';");
    if (!$result)
    {
      throw new RuntimeException('MySQL error');
    }

    if (mysql_num_rows($result))
    {
      $page_id = mysql_fetch_assoc($result);
      $parent_id = $page_id['id'];
      $page_ids[] = $page_id;
      unset($url_parts[$key]);
    }
```

```php
  else
  {
    break;
  }
}

// remaining URL parts are extra request parameters
$this->setExtraRequestParameters($url_parts);

while(empty($page_ids)
    || $page_ids[count($page_ids)-1]['skip_to_first_subpage'])
{
  $page_id = $this->find_first_subpage(
      $page_ids[count($page_ids)-1]['id']);
  $result = mysql_query("SELECT id, skip_to_first_subpage ".
  "FROM content WHERE id='$page_id';");
  if ($result && mysql_num_rows($result))
    $page_ids[] = mysql_fetch_assoc($result);
  else
    break;
}

$page = array();
foreach($page_ids as $id)
{
  $page = $this->get_page_info($id['id']);
  if ($page)
  {
    $uri_prefix .= '/'.$page['uri'];
    $this->breadcrumbs[] = array('id' => $page['id'],
    'uri' => $page['uri'], 'href' => $uri_prefix,
    'menu_name' => $page['menu_name'],
    'title' => $page['title']);
    if ($page['node']) $this->parent_node = $page['id'];

    $this->add_title_part($page['title']);
  }
```

```
    else
      break;
  }
  $this->page_url = $uri_prefix;
  $this->page = $page;
  $this->assign('breadcrumbs', $this->breadcrumbs);
  return true;
}

function redirect($page_id)
{
  if ($this->page['id'] != $page_id && $page_id > 0)
  {
    session_write_close();
    header('HTTP/1.1 301 Moved Permanently');
    header('Location: '.$this->get_url($page_id));
    exit;
  }
}

function open_page()
{
  $result = mysql_query("SELECT * FROM content c ".
    "WHERE id='{$this->page['id']}';");
  if ($result && mysql_num_rows($result))
  {
    $this->page = mysql_fetch_assoc($result);
    $this->page['contents'] = plain_text($this->page['contents']);

    if ($this->is_admin)
    {
      if (!$this->page['available_for_admins'])
      {
        $this->page['contents'] =
            TPL_NOT_AVAILABLE_FOR_ADMINS;
        $this->available = false;
      }
```

```
    else if ($this->cms_login->user['id'] != 1
        && !$this->page['available_for_guests']
        && !$this->page['available_for_users']
        && !$this->has_permission(
            $this->cms_login->user['id'],
            $this->page['id'])
            )
    {
      $this->page['contents'] =
          TPL_NOT_AVAILABLE_FOR_SPECIFIC_ADMIN;
      $this->available = false;
    }
}
else if ($this->is_user)
{
  if (!$this->page['available_for_users'])
  {
    $this->page['contents'] =
        TPL_NOT_AVAILABLE_FOR_USERS;
    $this->available = false;
  }
}
else
{
  if (!$this->page['available_for_guests'] && !$this->is_user)
  {
    $this->page['contents'] =
        TPL_NOT_AVAILABLE_FOR_GUESTS;
    $this->available = false;
  }
}
```

```php
    if (!$this->page['show_contents'])
    {
      $this->page['contents'] = TPL_INVISIBLE;
      $this->available = false;
    }
  }
  else
  {
    $this->page['contents'] = TPL_NOT_FOUND;
  }
}

function has_permission($admin_id, $page_id)
{
  $result = mysql_query("SELECT id FROM permissions WHERE ".
  "admin_id='$admin_id' AND page_id='$page_id';");
  if ($result && mysql_num_rows($result))
    return true;

  return false;
}

function find_first_subpage($parent_id = 0)
{
  $result = mysql_query("SELECT id FROM content WHERE ".
  "parent_id='$parent_id' ORDER BY priority ASC, id ASC;");
  if ($result && mysql_num_rows($result))
      return mysql_result($result, 0, 0);
}

function show_page()
{
  if ($this->available)
  {
    $this->cache_id = 'page_'.$this->page['id'];
    if ($this->page['include_file'] != "
        && file_exists(ROOT.'/site/'.$this->page['include_file']))
```

```php
    {
      include_once(ROOT.'/site/'.$this->page['include_file']);
    }
  }
  $this->menu = $this->load_menu();
  $this->assign('menu', $this->menu);
  $this->assign('page_id', $this->page['id']);
  $this->assign('site_title', $this->get_site_title());
  $this->assign('contents', $this->page['contents']);
  $this->assign('description', $this->page['description']);
  $this->assign('keywords', $this->page['keywords']);
  $this->assign('page_title', $this->page['title']);
  $this->assign('page_url', $this->page_url);

  $this->assign('subnavigation', $this->subnavigation());
  $this->assign('main_navigation', $this->main_navigation());
  $this->assign('is_admin', $this->is_admin);
  $this->assign('is_user', $this->is_user);
  $this->assign('parent_node', $this->parent_node);

  $this->assign('meta_title', $this->get_page_title(' - ', true));

  $this->assign('timers', sfTimerManager::getTimers());

  $this->smarty->caching = $this->caching;
  $this->smarty->display(
      ($this->template != " ?
          $this->template
          : $this->default_template),
          $this->cache_id);
}

function add_title_part($title_part)
{
  $this->title_parts[] = $title_part;
}
```

```php
function get_title_parts()
{
  return $this->title_parts;
}

function get_page_title($separator = ' - ', $reverse = false)
{
  $title_parts = $this->get_title_parts();

  if ($reverse)
  {
    $title_parts = array_reverse($title_parts);
  }

  return implode($separator, $title_parts);
}

function menuitems($parent_id=0, $uri_prefix='')
{
  $timer = sfTimerManager::getTimer('navigation');
  $timer->startTimer();

  $menu_items = array();
  $result = mysql_query("SELECT c.id, t.uri, t.menu_name ".
  "FROM content c ".
  "LEFT JOIN content_translations t ON c.id = t.content_id ".
  "WHERE ".
  "c.parent_id='$parent_id' AND c.show_in_menu='1' AND (".
  ($this->is_admin ? "c.available_for_admins='1' OR ":"") .
  ($this->is_user ?
      "c.available_for_users='1'"
      : "c.available_for_guests='1'").
      ") ORDER BY c.priority ASC, c.id ASC;")
          or $this->trigger_error(mysql_error());
```

```php
  if ($result && mysql_num_rows($result))
  {
    while ($item = mysql_fetch_assoc($result))
    {
      $item['href'] = $uri_prefix.$item['uri'];
      $menu_items[$item['id']] = $item;
    }
  }
  $timer->addTime();

  return $menu_items;
}

function load_menu()
{
  $menu = array();
  $menu[0] = $this->menuitems(0, '/');
  foreach($this->breadcrumbs as $item)
  {
    $menu[$item['id']] = $this->menuitems(
        $item['id'],
        $item['href'].'/'
          );
  }
  return $menu;
}

function subnavigation()
{
  if ($this->page['id'] != $this->parent_node
      && !empty($this->menu[$this->page['id']]))
    return $this->menu[$this->page['id']];
  else if ($this->page['parent_id'] != $this->parent_node
      && $this->page['parent_id'] != 0)
    return $this->menu[$this->page['parent_id']];
}
```

```php
function main_navigation()
{
  return $this->menu[$this->parent_node];
}

function get_uri_prefix($page_id)
{
  $uri_prefix = '/';
  if ($page_id > 0)
  {
    foreach ($this->breadcrumbs as $item)
    {
      $uri_prefix .= $item['uri'].'/';
      if ($item['id'] == $page_id) break;
    }
  }
  return $uri_prefix;
}

public function get_url($page_id)
{
  $timer = sfTimerManager::getTimer('get_url');
  $timer->startTimer();

  $url = '';
  while ($page_id > 0)
  {
    $result = mysql_query("SELECT c.id, c.parent_id, t.uri ".
    "FROM content c WHERE c.id='$page_id';");
    if ($result && mysql_num_rows($result))
    {
      $page = mysql_fetch_assoc($result);
      $url = '/'.$page['uri'].$url;
      $page_id = $page['parent_id'];
    }
```

```php
    else {
      break;
    }
  }

  $timer->addTime();

  return $url;
}
function get_site_title()
{
  $site_title = SITE_TITLE;
  foreach($this->breadcrumbs as $crumb)
  {
    if ($crumb['id'] == $this->page['id'])
      $crumb['title'] = $this->page['title'];
    if ($crumb['title'] != '')
      $site_title .= ' - '.$crumb['title'];
  }
  return $site_title;
}

public function connect_db()
{
  $this->db_connection = @mysql_connect(
      MYSQL_HOST,
      MYSQL_USER,
      MYSQL_PASSWORD);
  if ($this->db_connection)
  {
    $this->db = @mysql_select_db(MYSQL_DB);
    if (!$this->db)
```

```php
    {
      ?><p class="warning">Geen database.</p><?
      exit;
    }
  }
  else
  {
    ?><p class="warning">Geen verbinding.</p><?
    exit;
  }
}

function assign($name, $value)
{
  $this->smarty->assign($name, $value);
}

function trigger_error($message, $error_type=E_USER_WARNING)
{
  $this->smarty->trigger_error($message, $error_type);
  }
}
```

Index

A

Abstract Factory design
  pattern, 15–18
Abstraction, 37, 67
  A-metric, 240
  vs. concretion, 67, 75, 77–81
  decoupling using, 87–88
  degrees, 239, 243
  depending on, 38
  introducing, 71–72
  leaky, 37–38
  levels, 74–77, 82
  removing, 48
  stability, 237–239, 241–243
Abstractness, *see* Stable Abstractions
  principle
Acyclic Dependencies
  principle, 185–186, 191–205,
  209–210, 217
  cycles
    problematic, 194–197
  dependency inversion, 203–205
  pseudo-cycles, 198–200
  visualizing dependencies, 191–193
Adapter design pattern, 88, 91, 98–99, 208,
  215, 229–234
Architectural layers, 175

B

Backward compatibility, 119–127, 131–135
Business logic, 103, 181–182, 184, 222, 245,
  252, 254

C

Chain of Responsibility design
  pattern, 208–215
Cohesion, 112, 185
Collaborator classes
  mailer, 6
  message creation, 6
  responsibilities, 10
Common Closure principle, 10, 161,
  171–178, 180–182
Common Reuse principle, 145–184, 199,
  201, 230, 234, 246
Composition, 87–91, 122, 166, 187, 191
Coupling, 9, 10, 87, 114, 185–190, 202
  See also Temporal coupling

D

Decorator design pattern, 20–21
Decoupling, 87–88, 210, 215
  See also Coupling

M. Noback, *Principles of Package Design*, https://doi.org/10.1007/978-1-4842-4119-6

Printed in the United States
By Bookmasters